THE GOLDEN BOOK

ALL PARIS

NEW EDITION

BONECHI

PREFACE TO THE NEW EDITION

The first edition of this guide was published many years ago, when Paris, with its innovative attractions, its avant-garde architectural works, and its continually-evolving culture, was one of the world's liveliest and most creative capitals, in image and in fact.

Things got their start with Beaubourg and the Forum des Halles, works that launched Paris on a collision course with the Third Millennium. Then came the Louvre Pyramid, the Musée d'Orsay, the soaring spires of La Défense, many other monuments that are simply to numerous to be listed in their entirety, and—latest in the series—the Musée du Quai Branly.

Our books have always documented the city's great advances during its ongoing development, step by step, with updated texts and photos.

Today we are presenting a new edition that traces the changing face of Paris with new graphics and new texts and documentation of all the most recent restoration work on the various monuments.

Paris continues to grow and to change with time, and as it does we will continue to correct and update our publications—so as to always offer tourists and visitors a faithful portrait of the City of Light.

Editorial conception: Casa Editrice Bonechi
Publication manager: Giovanna Magi
Project and picture research: Sonia Gottardo
Cover: Sonia Gottardo
Make-up: Federica Balloni
Texts: Giovanna Magi
Editing: Federica Balloni, Patrizia Fabbri
Drawings: Stefano Benini

© Copyright by Casa Editrice Bonechi, Via Cairoli 18/b – Florence – Italy
E-mail: bonechi@bonechi.it

Diffusion: OVET-PARIS
13, rue des Nanettes
75011 Paris - Tél. 43 38 56 80

Printed in Italy by Centro Stampa Editoriale Bonechi, *Sesto Fiorentino.*

The photographs are the property of the Casa Editrice Bonechi *Archives, taken by*
Marco Bonechi, Gérard Boullay, Gianni Dagli Orti, Serena de Leonardis, Luigi Di Giovine,
Paolo Giambone, Vincent Gauvreau, Jean Charles Pinheira, Andrea Pistolesi.

Other contributors:
Art Archive/G. Dagli Orti: *pages 25 above, 37 above, 84 below;*
Vincent Gauvreau: *page 92;*
© Moulin Rouge®: *page 118 below;*
Ph. M. Newman/Ag. Tips Images: *page 34 below;*
© Foto Scala, Firenze: *pages 64 below (© 1990 Foto Scala, Firenze), 93 above (© 2007 Musée du Quai Branly/Scala, Firenze)*
and below (© 2006 Musée du Quai Branly, photo Nicolas Borel/Scala, Firenze), 107 above (© 1990 Foto Scala, Firenze).

The publisher will be grateful for information concerning the sources of photographs without credits
and will be pleased to acknowledge them in future editions.

ISBN 978-88-7009-191-5
www.bonechi.com

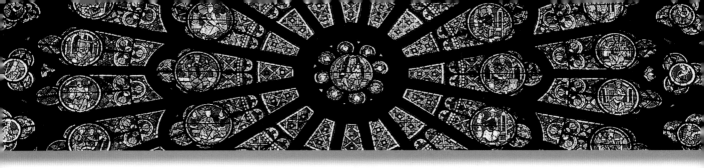

PARIS
history of the city

Paris was probably founded by the Gauls, who built a small settlement on the left bank of the Seine. The city is mentioned, with the name of Lutetia, by Julius Caesar who came here in 53 BC. As a result of the continual menace of barbarian invasions, the original settlement was moved to the Île de la Cité, and from there it expanded along the banks of the river. The residence first of the Merovingian and then of the Carolingian kings, Paris became a true capital in 987, when Hugues Capet, the first Capetian king, founded a new and powerful dynasty. One of Paris' moments of maximum splendor was between 1180 and 1223, when Philippe II Auguste came to the throne: construction of the Louvre was begun and the University was founded. During the reign of Louis IX "le Pieux" (Saint Louis, 1226-1270), the Sainte-Chapelle was built and work on the Notre-Dame cathedral continued. But the next dynasty, that of the Valois kings, brought wars and catastrophe, disorder and civil discord to Paris. Although Charles V briefly restored order, the fighting between the Armagnacs and Burgundians became more and more savage. England gained a foothold in France and in 1431 Henry VI was crowned king of France, in accordance with the terms of the Treaty of Troyes, by the English. In 1437, Charles VII reconquered Paris, but the population was exhausted by bloody revolts alternating with epidemics of the plague. Although throughout the 16th century the kings preferred to live in the castles of the Loire rather than in the capital, this did not end the internecine struggles in Paris itself. The spread of the Protestant religion created discord which for a long time rent Paris and the whole of France, culminating in the massacre of the Huguenots on the infamous night of St. Bartholomew (24 August 1572). After Henry III was assassinated in 1589, the city was besieged for four long years until finally it opened its gates to Henry IV, who had converted to Catholicism.

By the early 17th century, Paris counted about 30,000 inhabitants. The city became more and more important under the powerful Cardinal Richelieu and during the new dynasty of the Bourbon kings: by the time of Louis XIV, the Sun King, it had half a million inhabitants. But Paris earned its real place in history after 1789, the year of the French Revolution that was to mark the birth of the modern world. The long years of terror, in which many lives were lost and irreparable damage was done to many works of art, were forgotten in the splendor of the Empire and the dazzling court created by Napoleon, crowned emperor in 1804. From 1804 to 1814, Paris was constantly being enriched: the Arch of Triumph was built, the Vendôme column erected, and the Louvre enlarged. After the fall of the monarchies of Charles X and Louis-Philippe Bourbon-Orléans, the Second Republic was born and then Napoleon III took the throne. He entrusted the task of replanning the city to Baron Haussmann: the markets of Les Halles were built, the Bois de Vincennes and Bois de Boulogne laid out, the Opéra erected, and the great boulevards, typical expression of this historical era, were opened up. The year 1871 marked a new and sad page in the history of Paris with the Commune (18 March-28 May). Many splendid historic buildings were lost in these days of rebellion and destruction by fire: among others, the Hôtel de la Ville and the Tuileries palace. But Paris had new moments of splendor at the beginning of the 20th century, with the World Exhibitions, the construction of the Grand Palais and the Petit Palais, and the birth of important movements of art, painting and literature. Unfortunately the city had yet to suffer the bombardments and destruction of two long wars. During World War II it fell into the hands of the German Army in 1940 and was not liberated by the Allies until 1944. But from that moment until today, as a city finally alive and free, Paris has resumed its place in the history of culture and humanity.

Welcome to Île-de-la-Cité

The splendid, stern cathedral of Notre-Dame dominates Île-de-la-Cité, reflecting in the waters of the Seine.

Notre-Dame

Built on the site of a Christian basilica which had been occupied previously by a temple dating from Roman times, the church was begun in 1163 under Bishop Maurice de Sully, work commencing from the choir. As time passed the nave and aisles followed, and finally the facade was completed in about 1200 by Bishop Eudes de Sully, though the towers were not finished until 1245. The builders then turned to construction of the chapels in the aisles and in the choir, under the direction of the architect Jean de Chelles. In about 1250 another facade, that of the north arm of the transept, was completed, while the facade on the south arm was begun some eight years later. The church could be said to have been finished in 1345. With the ravages of time and damages caused by men and by numerous tragic wars, the church's original appearance changed over the centuries, especially during the Revolution: in fact, in 1793 it ran the risk of being demolished. Notre-Dame at that point was dedicated to the Goddess of Reason, when Robespierre introduced this cult.

But it was reconsecrated in 1802, in time for the pomp and ceremony of the coronation of Napoleon I by Pope Pius VII in 1804. It underwent a definitive restoration by Viollet-le-Duc between 1844 and 1864, although it was threatened with destruction by fire in 1871. Imposing and majestic in its stylistic and formal consistency, the facade of Notre-Dame is divided vertically by pilasters into three parts and also divided horizontally by galleries into three sections, the lowest of which has three deep portals. Above this is the so-called Gallery of Kings, with twenty-eight statues representing the kings of Israel and of Judea. The Parisian people, who saw in them images of the hated French kings, pulled down the statues in 1793, but during later restoration they were returned to their original places. The central section has two grandiose mullioned windows on either side of the rose window, which dates from 1220-1225 and is nearly 33 feet in diameter. This central section is also adorned by statues of the Madonna and Child and angels in the center and of Adam and Eve at the sides. Above this runs a gallery of narrow, intertwined arch motifs, linking the two towers

Eugène Emmanuel Viollet-le-Duc (Paris 1814 – Lausanne 1879) was an architect specialized in restoration of medieval buildings and author of such works as the *Dictionary of French Architecture from the 11th to the 16th Century*, in ten volumes, and the *Dictionary of French Furnishings* (from the Carolingian period through the Renaissance), in six volumes. His work was and remains highly controversial, since he always strove to apply the principle that restoration is a "means to reestablish [a building] to a finished state, which may in fact never have actually existed at any given time." And for this reason, many of the buildings he "restored" were considerably modified, if not reinvented outright. For Notre-Dame, Viollet-le-Duc designed and built the *flèche* (a type of spire) over the center dome of the church, further embellished the embrasures of the portals with new statues, and rebuilt the Gallery of Kings that had been lost during the Revolution. He left his "signature" in the face of one of the statues.

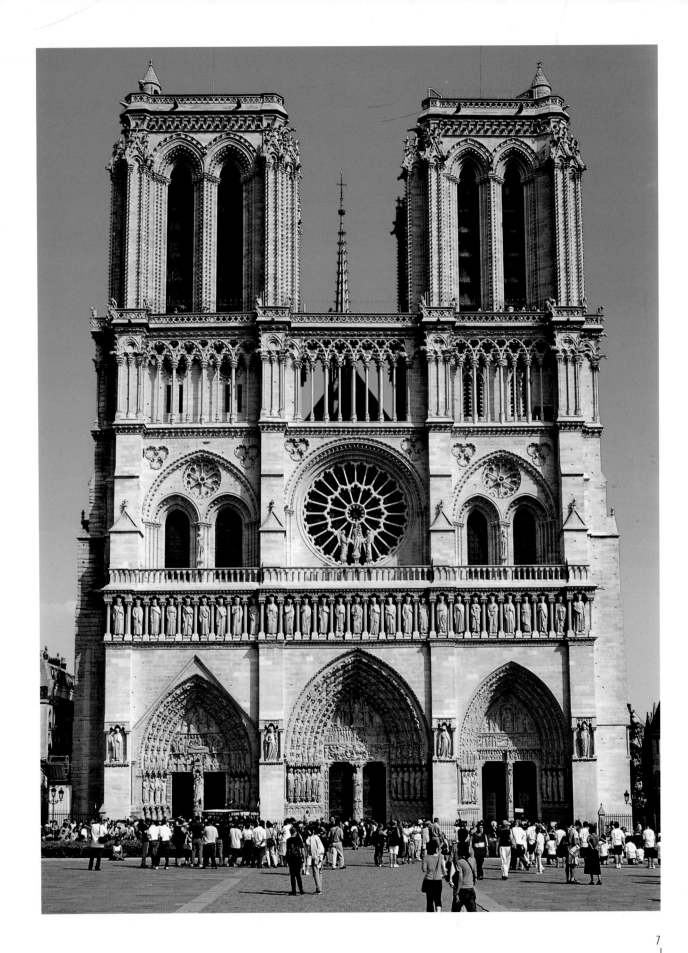

The portals and the statues

The Gothic style of these portals (dating to about 1220) is characterized by a softer and more direct way of looking at and interpreting nature, whereby the material is used to create more delicate forms and the space between one figure and another is more freely distributed. On the central portal is the subject perhaps best loved by the Gothic artists; that is, the Last Judgment. On the pilaster which divides it in two is the figure of Christ, while on the embrasures are panels with personifications of the Vices and Virtues and statues of the Apostles. Figures depicting the celestial court, Paradise and Hell are sculpted with great skill around the curve of the arch. The lunette with the Last Judgment is divided into three sections and is dominated by the figure of Christ, at whose sides are the Madonna, St. John and angels with symbols of the Passion. Beneath this on one side are the blessed who have merited salvation, and on the other side the damned being dragged towards their final punishment. In the lower strip is the Resurrection. The right-hand portal, called the Portal of St. Anne and built between 1160 and 1170, has reliefs dating to the 12th and 13th centuries, with a statue of St. Marcel, bishop of Paris in the 5th century, on the pilaster which divides it. In the lunette Our Lady is depicted between two angels and on the two sides are Bishop Maurice de Sully and King Louis VII. The third portal, the one on the left, is called the Portal of the Virgin and is perhaps the finest of the three because of its epic tone and the solemn grandeur of its sculpture. On the dividing pilaster is a Madonna and Child, a modern work. In the lunette above are subjects dear to the iconography of the life of the Virgin, including her death, glorification, and Assumption. At the sides of the portal are figures depicting the months of the year, while in the embrasures are figures of saints and angels.

at the sides. The towers were never completed, but even without spires, they have a picturesque and fascinating quality with their tall mullioned windows.

Entering the **interior** of the cathedral, one is immediately struck above all by its dimensions: no less than 130 meters long, 50 meters wide and 35 meters high, it can accommodate as many as 9000 persons. Cylindrical piers 16 feet in diameter divide the church into five aisles, and there is a double ambulatory around the transept and choir. A gallery with double openings runs around the apse above the arcades, surmounted in turn by the ample windows from which a tranquil light enters the church. Chapels rich in artworks from the 17th and 18th centuries line the aisles up to the transverse arm of the transept. At each end of the transept are rose windows containing splendid stained glass pieces dating from the 13th century; particularly outstanding is the stained glass window of the north arm, dating to about 1250, with scenes from the Old Testament and a Madonna and Child in the center, justly celebrated for the marvelous blue tones which it radiates. From the transept one passes into the choir, at the en-

The **south rose window**, constructed in 1260 ca. and restored during the 18th century, is located on the south side of the cathedral and is made of 84 medallions in four circles. It depicts apostles, bishops, martyrs, and angels, and such Bible scenes as the Judgment of Solomon, the Annunciation, and the Flight into Egypt. At the center, a Blessing Christ; in the lower corners, six medallions represent the Descent into Limbo (left) and the Resurrection (right). Almost an iconographic extension of the rose window, the group of 16 prophets represented in the tall paired windows that open underneath; the originals were modified by Gérente under the direction of Viollet-le-Duc.

The monsters of Notre-Dame

Medieval French legend roils with fantastic monsters, the same that, sculpted in stone, perching on a spire or peeking out over a wall, watch Paris from the Galerie des Chimères that links the north and south towers of Notre-Dame. Gargoyles and chimeras of biblical and pagan origin, with shadowy demonical overtones. In truth, the onomatopoeic French *gargouille* is a spout projecting from a roof gutter to throw rainwater clear of a building. And since these functional elements on the facade of Notre-

trance to which are two piers; the north pier has the famous statue of Notre-Dame-de-Paris, dating to the 14th century and brought here from the Chapel of St. Aignan. An 18th-century carved wooden choir surrounds half of the presbytery, and on the high altar is a *Pietà* by Nicolas Coustou; to its sides are two more statues, one representing Louis XIII by Guillaume Coustou and the other Louis XIV by Coysevox. Finally there is the am-

Left, the majestic interior of the cathedral. On this page, the rose window and the apse, with the fountain of the Virgin in Place Jean XXIII.

From the bridge called Pont de la Tournelle, constructed in 1370 but rebuilt many times, one can see the vast curve of the **apse of Notre-Dame**. In other churches, the part centering on the apse usually aims at gathering together, as if in an embrace, all the lines of force and the rhythmic and spatial values of the interior. But here the apse creates its own rhythm, serving as a terminal point but also creating a new sense of movement that extends to every structural element, from the rampant arches to the ribbing. The rampant arches, which here reach a radius of nearly 50 feet, are the work of Jean Ravy.

Dame were carved in the shape of monsters, winged dragons, and bestial beings, the term now applies to any grotesquely carved figure. As for the chimeras, animals as fantastic as the gargoyles and found on the west facade as well, their role is exclusively decorative. Although they derive directly from the innumerable, richly illustrated medieval bestiaries, these creatures on the towers and facades of Notre-Dame are creatures of the architectural fantasy of Viollet-le-Duc, who added them when the cathedral was restructured, to create an unreal galaxy of demons that observe the city with irony and a concerned air.

bulatory, with radial chapels containing numerous tombs. On the right, between the Chapelle Saint-Denis and the Chapelle Sainte-Madeleine, is the entrance to the Treasury, displaying relics and sacred silverware. Among the most important relics are a fragment of the True Cross, the Crown of Thorns, and the Sacred Nail. At this point, having reached the end of the church, if one turns towards the main entrance one cannot help being struck by the great rose window above the 18th-century organ.

The sites of a great romance
Published in 1831 and set in the year 1482, *Notre-Dame de Paris* (*The Hunchback of Notre Dame*) is a masterwork by Victor Hugo that narrates the story of the doomed love between the hunchback Quasimodo and the beautiful gypsy Esmeralda, complicated by the insane, evil passion harbored by the Archdeacon of the Cathedral, Frollo, for the young woman. Quasimodo, desperate over Esmeralda's execution, kills Frollo and in turn dies, cradling Esmeralda's body in his arms. The novel is a grandiose evocation of the Paris of the late Middle Ages, with two great protagonists: the church, and Quasimodo.
The story, set in the shadow of the massive cathedral, has never ceased to tweak the imagination of directors, and the dramatic story of the hunchback and the gypsy has been transposed for the screen numerous times. The first film, released in 1923, was silent and starred Lon Chaney. The 1939 edition, a masterpiece by William Dieterle, starred the great Charles Laughton in the role of Quasimodo and Maureen O'Hara as Esmeralda. The third film, from 1956, starred Anthony Quinn and Gina Lollobrigida. The story has even been made into an animated feature by Disney, and produced as a musical with score by Riccardo Cocciante.

The Cathedral of Notre-Dame

The north and south towers symmetrically frame the majestic west facade of the cathedral. The north tower, originally the church's sole bell tower, is equipped with four 19th-century bells.

A huge, brightly-colored rose window illuminates the west facade. Below the window, the noteworthy organ with its 8000 pipes, some of which are medieval originals.

The south transept, the perfect mirror image of its opposite number to the north, opens with an enormous rose window, 13 meters in diameter, that lights the interior of the cathedral.

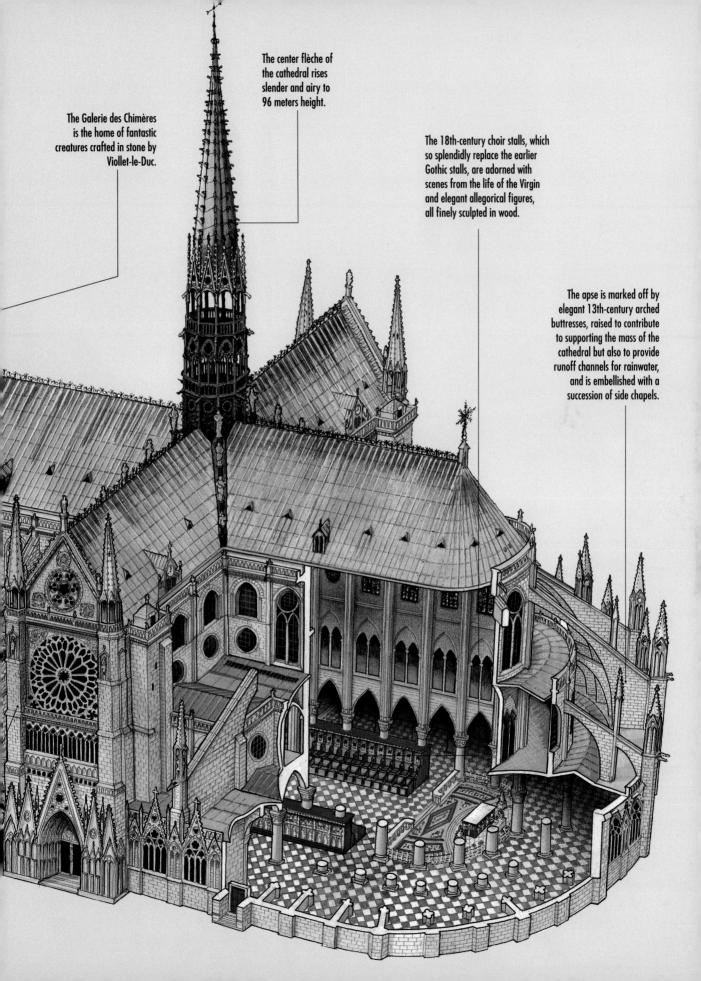

The Galerie des Chimères is the home of fantastic creatures crafted in stone by Viollet-le-Duc.

The center flèche of the cathedral rises slender and airy to 96 meters height.

The 18th-century choir stalls, which so splendidly replace the earlier Gothic stalls, are adorned with scenes from the life of the Virgin and elegant allegorical figures, all finely sculpted in wood.

The apse is marked off by elegant 13th-century arched buttresses, raised to contribute to supporting the mass of the cathedral but also to provide runoff channels for rainwater, and is embellished with a succession of side chapels.

The Bouquinistes

Repeatedly banished from the area by royal decree, only in 1891 were these street-vendors legally permitted to open the shutters of their stalls in the shadow of Notre-Dame, with the proviso that they scrupulously respect their assigned spaces so that passersby would be free to look out over the Seine.

With a little luck, today's strolling shopper may find a rare book, a period photograph, or even an original poster of the Paris of past eras and the personalities who made the city's history.

Conciergerie

The Conciergerie building, with its twin towers flanking the entrance to Paris' oldest prison.

This severe, powerful building on the banks of the Seine dates to the time of Philip the Fair; that is, late 13th-early 14th century. Its name derives from *concierge*, as the royal governor in charge of the building was called. Today, it is a wing of the Palais de Justice. The visit to the palace is of considerable interest, since it carries the visitor back to distant times of conspiracy and intrigue at high levels of government, and much more. On the ground floor is the Hall of the Guards, with massive pillars supporting Gothic vaults, and the large Hall of the Men-at-Arms. The latter room, with four aisles, 68 meters long by 27 wide and an 8-meter ceiling, was originally the king's dining hall. But despite its royal heritage, the Conciergerie is most strongly associated, in popular imagination, with the French Revolution. The building was converted to a state prison in the 16th century; later, during the Revolution, its cells were occupied by thousands of citizens who lived out their last hours here before climbing the steps to the guillotine. For a fee, the prisoners could obtain a straw pallet on which to sleep in a large room on the ground floor, with cruciform vaults; the poor prisoners were quartered in another area with the tragically ironic name of Rue de Paris. The cell of Marie-Antoinette, converted into a chapel in 1816 by the only surviving daughter of Louis XVI, the Duchess of Angoulême, is perhaps the most evocative of all: the royal prisoner, scornfully called "that Austrian woman," was incarcerated here from 2 August until 16 October 1793, when, at 7 o'clock on that Wednesday morning, after cutting her own hair, she climbed on the executioner's cart to be taken to the same scaffold where her husband had died nine months earlier.

The Execution of Marie-Antoinette

On 16 October 1793, the public prosecutor of the Revolutionary Tribunal of Paris, Fouquier-Tinville, read the sentence by which "Marie-Antoinette of Austria, widow of Louis Capet" was condemned to death.

The last day of she who had been dubbed "Madame Deficit" began at four in the morning, when—without a flicker of emotion—she heard the judgment of conviction and returned to her cell to prepare for her last journey. Her camisole and petticoat were black; her dressing-gown, fichu, and mousseline bonnet, white. Her wrists were bound behind her back.

His queen, "that Austrian," made her last journey seated alone on a dirty wagon, exposed to the insults and derisive shouts of the people who lined the streets leading to the place of her execution.

At a window along Rue St-Honoré was the painter Jacques Louis David; a few strokes of his pencil have left us an unforgettable and cruel portrait-caricature of Marie-Antoinette, sitting erect, her face an impenetrable mask, her lips set in a tight, disdainful line. That which had been one of her most endearing characteristics—the charming pout typical of all the Hapsburgs—had been transformed into an expression of dark and total contempt for everything that surrounded her. This is the last official image we have of Marie-Antoinette: a broken and humiliated woman facing death with immense dignity.

Palais de Justice

The western sector of the Île-de-la-Cité is occupied by the Palais de Justice or Palace of Justice, a complex of buildings dating to various periods and, including the Conciergerie, the Sainte-Chapelle, and the Palace of Justice itself. The principal facade of the latter faces on the Boulevard du Palais, preceded by the scenic Cour de Mai with its elegant wrought iron railing. At the back of the Cour de Mai, to the right of the staircase, was the door of the Conciergerie through which passed the wagons with the 2600 prisoners condemned to the guillotine during the Reign of Terror.

Sainte-Chapelle

A vaulted passageway from the courtyard of the Palais de Justice leads to that masterpiece of Gothic architecture which is the Sainte-Chapelle. It was built for Louis IX (Louis the Blessed) to contain the relic of the crown of thorns which the king had bought in Venice in 1239 after it had been conveyed to that city from Constantinople. The architect who planned the chapel was probably Pierre de Montreuil, the architect of Saint-Germain-des-Prés; here he actually designed two chapels,

Boulevard du Palais offers the best panorama of the sumptuous facade and the superb gates of the Palais de Justice.

The interior of the Lower Chapel, with its polygonal apse.

The Upper Chapel looks almost like a larger-than-life reliquary, adorned with the delicate embroidery of its high arches and towering polychrome windows.

standing one above the other; they were both consecrated in 1248. The lower church acts as a high base for the overall structure, with large windows crowned with cusps above. The steep sloping roof is adorned by a slim and delicate marble balustrade, and this graceful piece of architecture is splendidly crowned by a slender openwork spire 65 meters high. Two more towers with spires stand on each side of the facade, in front of which is a porch; above the porch is a large rose window with cusps, dating to the end of the 15th century, illustrating the Apocalypse.

Lower Church. There is a sudden change of atmosphere, style, and emotion when one descends from the Upper to the Lower Chapel. Only 7 meters high, it has three aisles, but the nave is enormous compared to the two much smaller aisles at the sides. Trilobate arch motifs supported by shafts recur along the walls. The apse at the end is polygonal. But here, as in the Upper Chapel, color predominates. The rich polychrome decoration overshadows the architecture, which is thus transformed into a simple support for the decorative element.

Upper Church. Climbing a staircase from the Lower Chapel, one reaches the Upper Chapel, a splendid reliquary with the appearance of a precious jewel-case. Without aisles, it is 17 meters wide and 20 meters high. A high plinth runs all around the church, interrupted by perforated marble arcades which from time to time open into deep niches. In the third bay are the two niches reserved for the king and his family. On each pillar is a 14th-century statue of an Apostle.

The structure is lightened as much as possible to allow the huge stained-glass windows, nearly 15 meters high, to dominate the architectural composition. Whereas, in the Romanesque period, a church's paintings were usually half-hidden in an apse, in the curve of an arch, or under a wide vault, in this Gothic creation the artwork is magnificently transferred to the stained-glass windows: triumphantly presented, it illuminates the whole church with precious chromatic shadings. The fifteen 13th-century stained glass windows of the Sainte-Chapelle contain 1134 scenes and cover an area of 618 square meters; in splendid colors and in an almost feverish style, they illustrate Biblical and Evangelical scenes.

Pont Neuf

This is the most beautiful of the bridges over the Seine, and also the longest, with 330 meters of arches and spans crossing the two channels of the river at Île-de-la-Cité. And despite its name, it is also the oldest of Paris' bridges, built between 1578 and 1606. Nevertheless, its conception makes it a modern bridge, revolutionary in comparison to previous designs. All the other city bridges were in fact flanked by tall buildings that obstructed the view of the river. The Pont Neuf, instead, courted the prospective of the Seine, and the bridge, with its round arches, became an enormous balcony opening onto the river. The Parisians admired its beauty and immediately grasped its importance: the bridge soon became a venue for meeting or simply strolling. In the early 17th century, it was even a key player in the birth of the French comedy theater, since it was here that the famous Tabarin held his performances.

Statue of Henry IV

The equestrian monument portraying Henry IV was cast by the sculptor François Fréderic Lemot in 1818 to replace the original statue that Francavilla (pupil of Giambologna) had erected in 1614, four years after the death of the king. The first equestrian statue in Paris, it was toppled during the French Revolution in 1792.

SQUARE DU VERT-GALANT

Known by the nickname given to Henry IV, "Vert-Galant," this pleasant little enclosed garden is reached via a stairway behind the statue of the king. The square is at the very end of the Île, and the garden occupying the square thrusts out over the calm waters of the Seine like the bow of a ship plowing the waves.

The equestrian monument of Henry IV at the center of the Pont Neuf and a suggestive view of the Square du Vert-Galant from the Seine.

Pont des Arts

Also known as the *Passerelle des Arts*, this bridge unites the Louvre's Cour Carrée and the left bank of the Seine, where the Institut de France building stands. The bridge is 156 meters long and 9.80 wide.

Construction began in 1802, directed by the engineer Louis-Alexandre de Cessar, and continued for two years. Strictly reserved for pedestrian traffic and built of cast-iron, the walkway was embellished with plants and tubs of flowers so that it seemed almost a hanging garden; the impression was reinforced by its elevation over the Seine embankment. Like the other city spans, it was a toll bridge.

The bridge was closed for repairs in 1970 after a large barge collided with it. Since its original cast-iron was not restorable, it was rebuilt in steel in the period 1982-1984 in respect of the original forms, even though with two fewer spans.

Left, a view up one channel of the Seine toward the Pont Neuf. Bottom, a view of the Pont des Arts. Upwards of 65,000 Parisians strolled here on the day of the bridge's inauguration, and it is still a preferred spot for painters, offering as it does an exceptional view of the Louvre, the towers of Notre-Dame, and the spire of the Sainte-Chapelle.

Institut de France

Linked to the Louvre by the picturesque Pont des Arts, Paris' first iron bridge, this building was erected in 1665 as the result of a bequest by Cardinal Mazarin who in 1661, three days before his death, stipulated in his will that two million francs be spent on the construction of a college capable of accommodating 60 students, to be called the Collège des Quatre Nations. In 1806 Napoleon ordered the transfer here of the Institut de France, which had been formed in 1795 by the union of five academies: the Academies of France, of the Sciences, of Letters, of Fine Arts, and of Moral and Political Sciences. The facade of the central section has columns supporting a pediment, above which is a fine cupola with the insignia of Mazarin sculpted on its drum. This section is linked to the pavilions at either side by two curving wings with two orders of pillars. Facing each other across the courtyard are the Mazarin Library on the left and, on the right, the formal Meeting Room, where beneath the cupola, in what was originally the college chapel, new members of the Académie de France are installed with a solemn ceremony. In the vestibule preceding this room is the tomb of Mazarin, a work done by Coysevox in 1689.

Two images of the facade of the Institut de France, on which columns support a pediment.

Facing page: the facade of the Hôtel de Ville and details of the decoration over the entrance. The female figure above the clock is an allegory of the City of Paris, while above her are allegories of two rivers, the Seine and the Marne.

Hôtel de Ville

In the center of a huge square, for five centuries was the site of public executions, stands the venerable Hôtel de Ville, today the municipal headquarters of the city. The site was previously occupied by a 16th-century building, designed by Domenico da Cortona: built in the Renaissance style, it was destroyed by fire in 1871 during the struggles that led to the fall of the Commune. The later building thus takes its inspiration from this lost edifice. It was designed by the architects Deperthes and Ballu, who completed it in 1882. The complex is certainly imposing and original, with its various pavilions surmounted by domes in the shape of truncated pyramids and a forest of statues wherever one turns. In fact, there are no less than 136 statues on the four facades of the building, while on the terrace is the statue depicting Etienne Marcel, leader of the Parisian merchants and fomenter of the disorders which crippled Paris in the 14th century. Over the centuries the building has been the scene of important historical events. The most tragic of all, perhaps, took place on the morning of 27 July 1794, the day which in the new calendar created by the Republicans was called the 9th of Thermidor. Robespierre, the Incorruptible, was closed inside the Hôtel with his followers, trying to find a way to avoid a civil war he knew would certainly create havoc among the factions that had emerged within the Republican system. When the soldiers of the Convention burst into the room, he tried to commit suicide by shooting himself in the throat, but he succeeded only in inflicting a jaw wound. He was dragged off, to be executed the following day.

Tour Saint-Jacques

Erected between 1508 and 1522, it is 52 meters high and belongs to the most elaborate Gothic style. Narrow windows alternate with niches crowned by spires and pinnacles, embellished wuth many statues. The statue at the top of the tower of St. James the Greater is by Chenillon (1870). The tower is all that remains of the old church of Saint-Jacques de la Boucherie, one of the most important churches in Paris at the time, when it was the point of departure for pilgrimages directed to the sanctuary of Santiago de Compostela. The building was demolished in 1797 but the tower was left standing. Used for various experiments on the atmosphere carried out by Blaise Pascal (17th century physicist, mathematician, philosopher, and writer), it has served as an observatory for the metereological service since 1891.

Place des Victoires

This plaza, circular in form, was created in 1685 as the setting for the allegorical statue of Louis XIV made by Desjardins on commission from the Duke of Feuillade. Destroyed during the French revolution, the statue was replaced with another, in bronze, by Bosio. Unveiled on 25 August 1828, the work represented the king as a Roman emperor mounted on a rearing steed balanced by the flowing tail secured to the pedestal. For generations, Place des Victoires was a point of reference for the creative talents of the fashion world, who established their shops selling cashmere, laces, and bijoux here and in the adjacent streets. And the tradition continues, with Kenzo, Thierry Mugler, Cacharel, Blanc Bleu, and many other exclusive sales points.

The Tour Saint-Jacques and, bottom, the statue of Louis XIV at the center of Place des Victoires.

Place du Châtelet

This square takes its name from an ancient fortress built in wood by Charles the Bald in 870 as protection for the facing Pont au Change, the first bridge in Paris to permit access to Île-de-la-Cité. Rebuilt in stone in 1130 and renamed Grand Châtelet, the fortress became superfluous for defensive purposes following construction of Philippe Auguste's fortress but was converted for use as a prison. It was razed to the ground by Napoleon in 1808 to leave space for a new city square; at this time all the small streets surrounding the site, infested with profligates and criminals, were also suppressed. All that is left are the street names, which recall the activities once carried on in the quarter: Rue du Pied du Bœuf, Rue de la Triperie, Rue de la Tuerie.

The fountain now standing at the center of the square, its base decorated with sphinxes and statues, was erected in 1806-1808.

In 1860-1862, the architect Davioud, on commission from Baron Haussmann, built two theaters, one on each side of the square: the Théâtre du Châtelet (today the Théâtre Musical de Paris) and the Théâtre des Nations, which retained its original name from 1862 to 1949, to then become—until 1967—Théâtre Sarah Bernhardt, after the great French actress who directed the theater and played her most important roles there, above all *The Lady of the Camellias*. In 1968 it was renamed once again: Théâtre de la Ville.

The Châtelet fountain; top of page, several details and a depiction in a nineteenth-century painting by Etienne Bouhot, on display at the Musée Carnavalet.

Forum des Halles

The most animated, liveliest quarter of the city was defined by Emile Zola, with a colorful expression, as the "belly of Paris." Les Halles was in fact the site of the city's food market: ten pavilions in steel, iron, and cast-iron, construction of which began in 1854 to plans by Victor Baltard.

In 1969, the market was transferred to Rungis. Two years later, demolition of the enormous original pavilions began and on 4 September 1979 the new building, designed by the architects Claude Vasconi and Georges Pencreac'h, was inaugurated.

The Forum expresses a new concept of the urban space, in the shadow of the Gothic church of Saint-Eustache. It extends over more than 40,000 square meters with glass and aluminum structures, marble staircases and escalators, on four underground levels around a quadrangular open-air plaza.

Inside the Forum are boutiques selling clothing, objets d'art, food and drink specialties, and objects for the home; entertainment centers, restaurants, ten movie houses, banks, and information centers. Four Metro lines and two RAR lines serve the complex.

The Forum des Halles as it is today and as it once was, in a postcard of the early 20th century.

265 – PARIS – Les Halles le matin

Fountain
of the Innocents

In the form of a classical aedicule on a square ground plan, with arches at the sides and a frieze running along the pediments at the top, this fountain at the center of the tree-shaded square of the same name is one of the masterpieces of the French Renaissance. The delicate bas-reliefs which decorate it, by Jean Goujon, depict nymphs, tritons, and marine allegories.

Originally, the fountain was set against a wall in the square, which from the late Middle Ages, contained the cemetery of the Innocents. In 1786 the cemetery was suppressed and after that the fountain, with the addition of the fourth side, was moved to its current central position.

Top: Around the Forum des Halles there is now a broad swath of green, with glass-and-iron structures whose lines and forms recall the typical industrial architecture of the early 20th century. Right, the Fountain of the Innocents.

Beaubourg
(Centre Georges Pompidou)

Beaubourg, with its daring architecture, is now a part of our culture and civilization. In 1969, an international call to tender was announced and 49 countries participated, with 681 projects: the winner was the plan presented by Renzo Piano and Richard Rogers. Begun in April 1972, the center was inaugurated by Giscard d'Estaing on 31 January 1977. The building, often described as an "urban machine," occupies an area of 100,000 square meters. The conception is revolutionary: all the structures normally placed inside a building, such as escalators, elevators, safety exits, and vertical ducts, are situated on the outside. This idea of the general evolution of spaces is continued on the inside: every expression of contemporary art is a part of our lives and should be accessible to everyone at any time. Beaubourg is not intended to be a museum, preserving works of art, but instead a place for meeting and exchanging ideas, between artists and the public, the public and the things, where everyone can move around freely and approach the principal expressions of contemporary art and culture. Some curious facts: Beaubourg is taller and longer than the Parthenon on the Athens acropolis (it is 42 meters high and 166 long); it weighs 15,000 tons (steel) compared with the 7000 (iron) of the Tour Eiffel; each type of external duct is painted a different color in relation to its function: blue for the air-handling system, yellow for electricity, red for transport, and green for water.
As part of new reorganization work, the Public Information Library now occupies the northern portion of the first lev-

el, all the second, and a part of the third: here, anyone can consult the 350,000 printed documents via 370 multimedia workstations, free of charge.
The sixth level is given over to the "Georges" restaurant and various temporary exhibits, while the fourth and fifth floors house the great National Museum of Modern Art.

Between Place Georges Pompidou and the tiny Rue du Cloître Saint-Merri is Place Igor Stravinsky (above), entirely occupied by a huge, brightly-colored fountain in which fantastic animals spurt and splash jets of water in all directions.

The Produce Exchange
(Bourse du Commerce)

The old wheat market built in 1765 by the provost of the traders, the Produce Exchange is nowadays an imposing circular building adorned with a monumental series of paired pilaster strips. The offices form a crown around the large inner hall topped by a dome in glass and steel. The 16th-century fluted column rising up near the Exchange comes from the palace of Catherine de' Medici and was used as an observatory by the royal astronomer Ruggieri. When the area between the Exchange building and the church of Saint-Eustache was redesigned, modern structures and public spaces were added and enriched by works of modern art such as *L'Ecoute* ("The Listener") by Henri de Miller, a colossal head which seems to be listening to what is happening in the area.

Saint-Eustache

Considered the most beautiful church in Paris after Notre-Dame, Saint-Eustache was quite a long time in the making: begun in 1532, it was terminated only in 1637. Built to a design by Lemercier, the church features an unusual pastiche of styles, with vaults in flamboyant Gothic flanking Renaissance decoration in the form of three superimposed orders of soaringly-proportioned columns. The interior is 100 meters in length, 44 wide, and 33 high, with five aisles, a transept, and a choir. One of the chapels in the choir houses the tomb of Colbert, the famous Minister of Finance who served under Louis XIV: the sepulcher was designed by Le Brun, Coysevox sculpted the statues of Colbert and the exquisite *Abundance*, while Tuby is the author of the statue of *Fidelity*.

Snuggling against the church is Place René Cassin (named for the President of the European Court of Human Rights and winner of the Nobel Peace Prize in 1968), at the center of which stands the statue entitled *L'Ecoute* by Henri de Miller (1953-1999), also the designer of the sundial in the garden. The 70-ton sandstone *L'Ecoute* represents a colossal inclined head resting on a hand. The square, instead, was designed by the architect and town planner Louis Arretche, also the author of the recent Pont Charles de Gaulle.

Preceding page, the Bourse du Commerce building and
the modern sculptures that stand in the garden in front.

Saint-Eustache: above, the exterior, right, the
stained-glass windows and the tomb of Colbert.

Place Vendôme

Another masterpiece by Jules Hardouin-Mansart (who earlier designed Place des Victoires), this square is named for the Duke of Vendôme, who had his residence here. The square was created between 1687 and 1720 to provide a setting for Girardon's equestrian statue of Louis XIV, which was destroyed, like so many others, during the Revolution. A perfect example of stylistic simplicity and austerity, the plaza is octagonal in form and surrounded by buildings with large arches on the lower floor; the facades of the buildings sport skillfully distributed pediments, crowned, on the roofs, by numerous dormer windows, so typical that some regard Place Vendôme as a synthesis of the spirit and style of Paris. Among the important buildings here today are the famous Hôtel Ritz at no. 15, the house where Chopin died in 1849, at no. 12, and the residence of Eugenia de Montijo before she became the wife of Napoleon III. In the center of the square stands the famous column erected by Gondouin and Lepère between 1806 and 1810 in honor of Napoleon I. Inspired by Trajan's Column in Rome, it is 145 feet high; around the

The Vendôme column, adorned with reliefs narrating the exploits of Napoleon.

29 PARIS. — La Place Vendôme.

shaft is a spiral series of bas-reliefs, cast from the 1200 cannons captured at Austerlitz, in which the sculptor Bergeret narrated Napoleon's exploits. The column was originally topped by a statue of Napoleon; in 1814, this statue was destroyed and replaced by a likeness of Henry IV. In 1863, Napoleon "usurped" Henry, but eight years later, at the time of the Commune (when the voice of the great painter Gustave Courbet had a decisive say), this statue was also removed. Three years later, it was replaced once and for all by another replica of Napoleon.

Place Vendôme, the drawing-room of Paris

Since the time of the Second Empire, Place Vendôme has been a synonym of luxury, vanity, and—why not?–magic. The come-hither spell cast by the shop windows of its world-famous jewelers is irresistible and a walk around the square has become a "must" with all the connotations of an almost formal rite. The doors of the various *maisons* open on elegant interiors where velvets and boiseries create subdued settings for a unique kind of shopping. As early as 1700, Chaumet was creating jewels for the European courts: theirs is the parure set in rubies and diamonds that the founder Marie-Etienne Nitot fashioned for the marriage of Napoleon I and Marie Louise of Austria; theirs is the tiara, made using the crown jewels, given by the French emperor to Pope Pius VII. The collection of royal diadems is displayed in the singular museum in the Hôtel St James, where the boutique is also located. Since 1946, Place Vendôme also hosts the show-windows of Mauboussin, one of whose most famous pieces is the bracelet with a cabochon emerald given by Charles Chaplin to Paulette Goddard (when she was excluded from the cast of *Gone with the Wind*). Then there are the show windows of Mikimoto, with their extremely rare black pearls, and those of the Italians Bulgari and Buccellati. Separated in time by about ten years the one from the other (1893 and 1906, respectively) were the openings, on the square, of the *maisons* of Boucheron and of Van Cleef & Arpels, who brought extraordinary innovations to the field of jewellery. Other stopping-places include the elegant windows of the Italian Repossi and the Russian Alexandre Reza, with his pronounced preference for big stones, before turning off into the Rue de la Paix, the realm of Cartier, the world's best-known jeweller, he whom the English king Edward VII defined as "the jeweler of kings, the king of jewelers." But how can we abandon this square without having spared at least a glance for the Hôtel Ritz, the hundred-year chronicle of which is linked to so many great events in the history of Paris? The Hôtel Ritz was created in 1898 by the Swiss César Ritz, whose stated intent was to assure to the rich clientele of his establishment "all the refinement that a prince could desire in his own home." And thus he transformed the palace of the Duke of Lauzun at no. 15 Place Vendôme into that which was to become one of the world's premier hotels. Or, if nothing else, the most famous. Guests at the Ritz have included writers and politicians, movie stars and crowned heads, intellectuals and Arab princes, industrial magnates and financial tycoons. Marcel Proust wrote a part of his *Remembrance of Things Past* here; for the Dukes of Windsor was reserved a "fairy-tale" suite; Coco Chanel, who lived in an apartment here for 35 years, may have taken her inspiration for the face of her famous *Première* watch from the magical form of the square below her windows.

Opéra Garnier

With the Opéra Bastille, the Opéra Garnier is one of the two home theaters of the Opéra National de Paris; today, with its huge stage capable of hosting up to 450 artists, it is mainly a venue for ballet performances. It is probably Paris' most interesting building from the era of Napoleon III. Built to plans by Garnier in 1862-1875, the facade of the theater is distinguished by the profusion of decorative elements that was characteristic of the style of the time. The interior is all pomp and splendor, with the splendid main foyer, the grand staircase in precious marbles, the vault decorated by Isidore Pils, and of course the auditorium, with its marvelous ceiling paintings by Chagall (1964) depicting a sort of Olympus paying homage to 14 composers and their works, from *Tristan and Isolde* to the *Magic Flute*, from the *Firebird* to *Boris Godounov*, from *Swan Lake* to *Giselle*. The center disc evokes *Carmen* by Bizet, *La Traviata* by Verdi, *Fidelio* by Beethoven, and *Orpheus and Eurydice* by Gluck.

The Phantom of the Opera

1911 was the date of publication of the novel *Le Fantôme de l'Opéra* (*The Phantom of the Opera*) by Gaston Leroux, who took his inspiration from a legend then circulating in French theatrical circles that narrated how a deformed creature guilty of numerous crimes committed in the theater lived underneath it among tunnels and subterranean lakes. The novel was extraordinarily popular and, under the name *The Phantom of the Opera*, has been represented many times in film and on the stage. The latest, in order of time, is the famous musical version by Andrew Lloyd Webber, still staged by road companies in theaters throughout the world.

Palais Garnier

The sculptural group by Millet that triumphs at the summit of the facade of the Opéra Garnier theater building depicts Apollo raising his lyre.

The *winged horses* to the sides of *Apollo* are further sculptural masterpieces by Millet.

The distinctive flattened dome over the auditorium of the theater.

In the auditorium, with its 20-meter ceiling, the gleaming opulence of the elegant gilded decoration and the intense red of the velvet-upholstered seats set off the magnificent chandelier and the ceiling, painted by Marc Chagall with scenes from famous operas and ballets.

The enormous auditorium can hold more than two thousand spectators.

The monumental grand staircase, all agleam with polychrome marbles in white, green, and red, leads to the auditorium and the foyers.

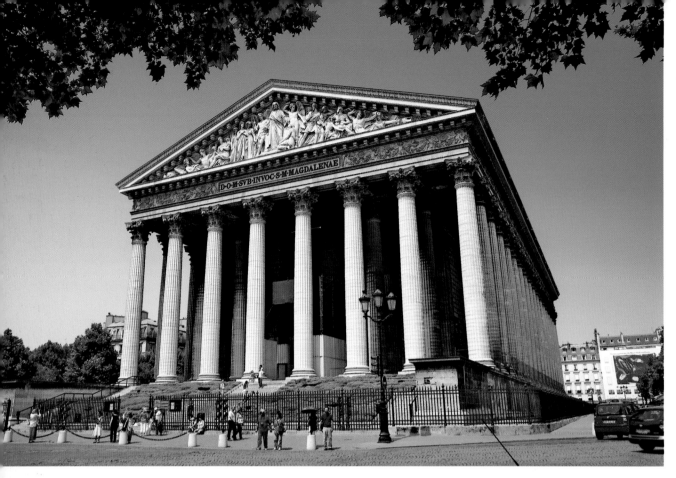

La Madeleine

It was Napoleon who wanted to erect a monument in honor of the Great Army, built along the lines of the Maison Carrée at Nîmes. To do so, he had a previous structure, which was not yet complete, totally demolished; work was resumed from scratch in 1806, under the direction of the architect Vignon. In 1814 it became a church dedicated to St. Mary Magdalene, standing in the center of the square of the same name. It has the form and structure of a classical Greek temple: a high base with a large stairway in front, a colonnade with 52 Corinthian columns 20 meters high running round the outside of the structure, and a pediment with a large frieze sculpted by Lemaire in 1834, representing the *Last Judgment*. The interior is aisleless, with a vestibule, in which are two sculptural groups by Pradier and Rude, and a semicircular apse. Above the high altar is the *Assumption of Mary Magdalene* by the Italian artist Marocchetti.

The church of the Madeleine as it is today and in postcards from the early 20th century. Top right, the interior of the church as designed by Constant d'Ivry in a painting by Pierre-Antoine Demachy (1723-1807), now in the Musée Carnavalet.

In front of the Madeleine, **Rue Royale** stretches out in fine perspective, closed at the other end by the symmetrical mass of Palais Bourbon. Rue Royale, opened in 1732, is short but full of luxury: at no. 3 is the celebrated **Maxim's** restaurant, with its Art Nouveau interiors; at no. 11 the crystal of **Lalique**; at no. 12 the silver of **Christofle**; at no. 16, for the sweet-toothed, the famous **Ladurée** pastry-shop. About halfway along Rue Royale is another important street, **Rue du Faubourg St. Honoré**, of which the number 13 was removed by order of the superstitious Empress Eugénie. This street has become almost synonymous with elegance and fashion, since it contains some of the most famous shops for perfumes, jewelry, and dresses in the world. Among their names are St-Laurent, Hermès, Cardin, Lancôme, Helena Rubinstein, Carita, and Lanvin.

Place des Pyramides

The tiny Place des Pyramides is located along Rue de Rivoli, near the Pavillon de Marsan. In 1874 it became the home of an equestrian statue of Joan of Arc by Emmanuel Frémiet: symbol of the national reconquest, the square has become a place of pilgrimage for the Realist parties.

Rue de Rivoli

This street, parallel to the Seine, connects Place de la Concorde to Place de la Bastille. It is one of Napoleon's greatest urbanistic successes–by two architects of the empire, Percier and Fontaine–but it was only completed during the reign of Louis-Philippe. In the section that skirts the Tuileries and the Louvre, an elegant portico with numerous shops lines one side.

Two close-ups of the equestrian statue of Joan of Arc and, right, two views of Rue de Rivoli. Under the arcades of this famous street are the entrances to great hotels, like the Meurice, and prestigious shops, including Paris' first English-language bookstore, the Librairie Galignani, inaugurated in 1800.

St-Germain-l'Auxerrois

In front of the eastern part of the Louvre is a small square dominated by the symmetrical facades of the Mairie, or town hall, of Paris's First Arrondissement, dating from 1859, and of the church of St-Germain-l'Auxerrois. The two buildings are separated by a bell-tower, built in the neo-Gothic style in 1860. Also called the "Grande Paroisse", the Great Parish Church, because it was the royal chapel of the Louvre in the 14th century, St-Germain-l'Auxerrois stands on the site of a sanctuary from the Merovingian era. Construction began in the 12th century and continued until the 16th. On the facade is a deep porch built between 1435 and 1439 in Gothic style, with five arches, each one different, their pillars adorned by statues. Other statues, depicting saints and kings, are in the three portals.

Palais Royal

This palace, built by Lemercier between 1624 and 1645, was originally the private residence of Cardinal Richelieu, who bequeathed it on his death in 1642 to Louis XIII. Today the seat of the Council of State, it has a colonnaded facade erected in 1774 and a courtyard that leads, through a double colonnade, into the beautiful and famous garden. Planned in 1781 by Louis, the garden extends for nearly 225 meters, with green elms and lime-trees and a profusion of statues. It is surrounded on three sides by robust pillars and a portico which today accommodates interesting shops selling antiques and rare books. During the Revolution it was a meeting-place for patriots: here the anti-monarchist aristo-

crats, among them the Duke of Orléans who was later rebaptised Philippe Egalité, met to discuss the state of the country and the historical developments about to be unleashed. In these gardens, in front of the Café Foy to be exact, Camille Desmoulins harangued the crowd on 12 July 1789, inflaming them with his passionate speech. Later, he tore a green leaf from one of these trees and put it in his hat as a cockade. The crowd followed his example and two days later, at the storming of the Bastille, many wore the leaf emblem.

Here and on the following pages: the court of honor of the Palais Royal is an example of the still-controversial integration of modern art into a Classical context. The placement, in the plaza, of Daniel Buren's columns and Pol Bury's fountains is still hotly debated. The first work, comprising white-and-black striped columns distributed over a 3000 square meter surface and illuminated at night by fluorescent green light, was installed in 1985. The same year saw the inauguration of two fountains in the form of moving stainless steel globes by the Belgian artist Pol Bury (1922-2005), considered one of the founding fathers of Kinetic Art.

The Grand Louvre

The Louvre dates back to 1200, when Philip Augustus had a fortress built near the river for defense purposes: it occupied more or less a fourth of today's Cour Carrée. The fortress was not, then, the royal residence (the king, in fact, preferred living in the Cité) but it housed, among other things, the royal treasure and the archives. In the 14th century, Charles V the Wise made fortress more habitable and took it as his residence. One of his additions was the famous Librairie. After his reign the Louvre was not used as the royal residence again until 1546, when Francis I commissioned the architect Pierre Lescot to improve it and adapt it to the new Renaissance tastes. He had the old fortress demolished and began the construction of the southwest wing of what is now the Cour Carrée. Work continued under Henry II. After his death, Catherine de' Medici entrusted Philibert Delorme with construction of the Tuileries Palace and a great gallery flanking the Seine to join it to the Louvre. Interrupted at Delorme's death, work continued under Henry IV and the Great Gallery and the Pavillon de Flore were completed. Enlargement continued under Louis XIII and Louis XIV; the architects Lemercier and Le Vau gave the Cour Carrée its present form; Claude Perrault was commissioned to build the east facade with its colonnade. When the court moved to Versailles in 1682, work on the Louvre was almost totally abandoned: the palace became so rundown that in 1750 it was suggested it be demolished.

We might say that the Louvre was saved by the women of Paris' markets when they marched on Versailles on 6 October 1789 to bring the royal family back to Paris. After the tumultuous years of the Revolution, Napoleon I finally resumed work on the Louvre; his architects, Percier and Fontaine, began the north wing along the Rue de Rivoli. It was finished, along with several other projects to complete the Louvre, following an 1852 decree by Napoleon III. When the Tuileries burned during the siege of the city in May of 1871, the Louvre acquired its breathtaking vista up the Champs-Elysées.

Ieoh Ming Pei was born in Canton, China, in 1917, and became a U.S. citizen in 1955. After his graduation from the prestigious M.I.T., he continued his studies at Harvard under Breuer and Gropius. His works are characterized by use of abstract forms and materials such as stone, glass, and steel, bound by a flair for technological daring and the theatrical. His most famous works, besides the Louvre Pyramid, are the John Hancock Tower in Boston, the Bank of China Tower in Hong Kong, and the east National Gallery building in Washington. In 1983, Pei was awarded the coveted Pritzker Architecture Prize.

The Louvre Pyramid by I. M. Pei is 21 meters high, set off by seven pools and fountains, and flanked by three lower pyramids that illuminate the entrances to the three wings of the museum: Sully, Denon, and Richelieu.

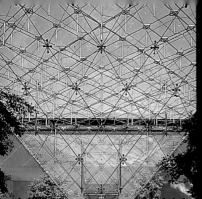

Top left: the Pyramide Inversée at the center of the Rond Point in front of the Louvre.
Bottom left: the Guichets du Carrousel give access from the Pont du Carrousel to the Rond Point and then the Guichets du Louvre. The term *guichet* means "counter" or "window" but the name is now commonly applied to the passageways that cut through the Louvre.

Top center: the bronze copy of the equestrian statue of Louis XIV that Bernini created while he was in Paris to present to the king his project for the Louvre palace–which was rejected.
Bottom center: the Richelieu Wing. Restructuring work has resulted in glass roofs for the Cour Puget, the Cour Marly, and the Cour Khorsabad, which evokes the Assyrian palace of Sargon II.

Top right: the Cour Marly is the ideal home for the famous *Marly Horses*, masterpieces by Guillaume Coustou (1745).
Cement copies have replaced the originals in Place de la Concorde.
Bottom right: the Pavillon Sully closes off the west end of the huge Cour Carrée, designed by the architects Lemercier and Le Vau.

THE MAJOR COLLECTIONS

ORIENTAL ANTIQUITIES – The Oriental Antiquities section, opened in 1881, displays a great number of finds from many archaeological sites in the area stretching from the Bosphorous to the Persian Gulf.

EGYPTIAN ANTIQUITIES – The celebrated Egyptian collection was founded by Jean-François Champollion, the archaeologist who first deciphered hieroglyphic writing. Continually enriched through acquisitions and donations, the Louvre collection is an enormous store of documentation on the civilization that developed along the banks of the Nile, from its furthest origins to the Ptolemaic, Roman, and Byzantine periods.

GREEK, ETRUSCAN, AND ROMAN ANTIQUITIES – Like the Egyptian collection, this section offers an extraordinary

panorama of artistic production from the archaic era of Greek civilization through the decline of the Roman Empire.

PAINTING COLLECTIONS – The Louvre picture gallery, certainly the première collection in all the world, was begun by Francis I (reigned 1515-1547).

SCULPTURE – As for sculpture, suffice it to say that the Louvre now offers the world's most comprehensive illustration of the history of sculpture, from its origins almost to our day.

APPLIED AND DECORATIVE ART – This section is of extraordinary importance from both the artistic and historic points of view. It embraces the most diverse objects, from furniture to tapestries, from jewelry to small bronzes, from miniatures to porcelain, and much much more.

Visir Seny-nefer (Senefer) and his wife Hatshepsut in a splendid example of surprisingly realistic Egyptian art. This sculptural group is of particular note for the excellent state of preservation of the colors and the extraordinary, skilful use of detail.

Seated Scribe, one of the Louvre's masterpieces of Egyptian statuary, carved in 2500 BC ca. Fifty-three centimeters in height, in painted limestone, the eyes encrusted with semiprecious stones, it was found in 1852 in Saqqara during a campaign conducted by Mariette.

Fragmentary colossus of Akhenaton. The Egyptian Antiquities section is linked to scientific research and digs conducted in Egypt. In 1826, Champollion, who four years earlier had deciphered the hieroglyphics, was appointed to organize a section specializing in Egyptian antiquities for the new Musée Charles X. The collection has never ceased to grow, with new acquisitions, donations, and finds from museum digs. This work is one in a long series of sandstone "colossi" representing the pharaoh and revealing his much-debated physical traits.

Discovered in 1820 by a peasant on the island of Milo in the Cyclades, this statue became the prototype of Greek female beauty. Slightly more than two meters tall, the **Venus de Milo** dates to the Hellenistic period (late 2nd cent. BC), but almost certainly derives from an original by Praxiteles, as indicated by the position of the figure, slightly unbalanced and almost leaning upon an imaginary support which makes her delicately twist and curve her torso inwards. The nude body of the goddess, endowed with lightness by the Parian marble, emerges from the folds of her garment as it slips downward, just barely held by the slightly bent left leg.

The **Victory** or **Nike of Samothrace** (from its find site), 2.75 meters high, is in Parian marble and dates to circa 190 BC when the inhabitants of Rhodes succeeded in winning several battles against Antioch III. The Nike stands erect on the prow of the ship which she will guide to victory: the impetuous sea wind strikes her with its full force, twisting the garments which cling to her limbs in an almost Baroque treatment of the drapery, and violently forcing her wings backwards.

LE TRESVICTORIEVX ROY DE FRANCE ·

CHARLES · SEPTIESME · DE CE NOM ·

This famous portrait of **Charles VII King of France** by Jean Fouquet seems to have been painted around 1444, in other words shortly after the painter's trip to Italy. The picture was given by the king to the Sainte Chapelle of Bourges. It entered the collections of the Louvre in 1838.

Portrait of Francis I by Jean Clouet, 1525 ca. Francis I, considered one of France's most magnificent and intelligent rulers, is shown in gala dress.

The Bathers, by Jean-Honoré Fragonard, was perhaps painted as the companion piece to another canvas depicting the same subject, now part of a private U.S. collection. Painted between 1756 and 1761, it is a hymn to life, to sensuality, to joy. Fragonard, pupil of Boucher, was the best-known and most highly-quoted exponent of the French Rococo style. The sensuality of the color and the fullness of the forms denote the influence of Rubens' style.

Diana Leaving Her Bath is one of the works most characteristic examples of the art of François Boucher, court painter at the time of Louis XV and a typical exponent of French Rococo. The female nudes he so loved to depict are always perfectly proportioned, triumphant in their adolescent nudity, and warm with soft, delicate color.

Portrait of Madame Récamier is an oil-on-canvas painted by Jacques-Louis David when his subject was 23 years old. It is therefore dated 1800, a period in which the great majority of David's production was celebratory. This splendid portrait is a marvelous exception, an image of great purity, acute psychological introspection, and pulsing humanity.

Gabrielle d'Estrées and Her Sister, the Duchess of Villars
portrayed in a work attributed to the Fontainebleau School, and is
datable to 1594-1596 ca. The two nudes are the sisters Gabrielle
d'Estrées and the Duchess of Villars. It is the latter who with a
symbolic gesture announces that her sister, favorite of King
Henry IV, will be giving birth to a son.

In this **Grande Odalisque** languidly resting on silk cushions, the
pure play of line so dear to Jean-Auguste Ingres (1780-1867) is
particularly evident: an antique statue seems to have come to life
and the body is endowed with a palpable humanity.

Painted in 1868 in the same pose as Leonardo's Mona Lisa, this splendid **Woman with a Pearl** is a sort of prototype of all the portraits by Camille Corot (1796-1875): a decisive and confident line, a calm light that envelops the entire figure and that sense of peace and serenity which characterize the great painter's style.

Shown at the Salon of 1827-1828, this canvas depicting **The Death of Sardanapalus** shows all the profound and intersecting influences that came to bear on its author, Eugène Delacroix (1798-1863), during his long stay in Spain and Morocco: the Oriental allure, the exaltation of the exotic and the mysterious, and the brilliant colors and the gleam of the gold tones that shine against the rich reds of the fabrics are clear testimony of these ascendancies.

Above left:
A fervent admirer of the new emperor, Jacques-Louis David (1747-1825) painted the enormous canvas depicting **The Coronation of Napoleon I** in 1805-1807. In it, he included not only the ceremony of 2 December 1804 in Notre-Dame, but also an extravagant total of 150 identifiable portraits, all equally vivid and solemnly respectful.

Below left:
The Kermesse is a lively composition that dates to the last period of Peter Paul Rubens (1577-1640) artistic life; that is, 1635 or 1638. And the influence of the country dances and outdoor feasts painted by Pieter Brueghel the Elder is eminently apparent.

Above:
Liberty Leading the People by Eugène Delacroix is a sort of political manifesto; in fact, it celebrates the events of 28 July 1830, when the population revolted and dethroned the Bourbon king. This canvas has been defined as the first political composition in modern painting.

This **Portrait of Charles I** is one of the many painted by Anthony van Dyck (1599-1641), pupil and collaborator of Rubens, for the English monarch who had called him to court and first appointed him official court painter and then dubbed him knight. In England, the artist—with his very personal language—inaugurated a tradition that produced many masters and prestigious masterpieces.

Inspired by the dramatic sinking of the French frigate *Medusa*, which in 1816 was carrying colonists to Senegal, this canvas by Théodore Géricault (1791-1824) was exhibited at the Salon in 1819. With its dramatic diagonal composition and its pyramid of intertwined, contorted bodies, **The Raft of the Medusa** is a work of crude realism but also of romantic pathos that paints a humanity in precarious equilibrium between hope and desperation.

After having succeeded his father Jean as court painter in 1540, François Clouet painted this portrait of **Elisabeth of Austria**, the young daughter of the Austrian Emperor Maximilian II, who married Charles IX King of France on 27 November 1570, with an exquisitely delicate use of color.

A classical example of the more relaxed and less distressing side of the art of Francisco Goya that we see in his prodigious production of court portraits. **The Countess del Carpio**, painted in 1794-1795, offers us the serene and delicate image of a self-possessed noblewoman whose slender figure, sumptuous black skirt, white lace mantilla, and large pink bow seem to materialize in relief against the background of a large empty space.

Above: **Portrait of an Old Woman** by Hans Memling (1433-1494). It would seem that this canvas was painted in 1470 or 1475. The subject is shown in a head and shoulders portrait posed before a landscape in accordance with the Flemish style already seen in the works of Van der Weyden. The painting was acquired by the Louvre in 1908 after it had passed through a number of private collections.

Above right: **The Moneylender and His Wife** by Quentin Metsys (1465-1530). This panel carries the inscription "Quinten matsys schilder, 1514": it is therefore attributable with certainty to that important Flemish painter who marked the transition from the Middle Ages to the Renaissance. Quentin Metsys is author of many altarpieces as well as profane subjects.

Below right: **The Beggars** by Pieter Brueghel the Elder (1525-1569). Of all of Brueghel's works, this wooden panel, signed and dated 1568, is the very smallest (18 x 21 cm). It has been given various interpretations, but it is most probable that Brueghel was sketching a universal satire of humanity, surely divided into social classes but just as surely brought together by suffering.

Leonardo began painting **The Virgin of the Rocks** in 1483 and completed the work in 1490 ca. In 1625, the painting was mentioned as being in Fontainebleau; it was perhaps part of a group of Leonardo's works purchased by Francis I. The light, emanating from the bottom of the composition, penetrates the rocks to illuminate the pyramidal structure of the group in the foreground.

Mona Lisa: there is really nothing left to say or to write about this masterpiece by Leonardo. Over time, this exquisitely gentle portrait of a girl has been an aesthetic, philosophical, and even advertising symbol, not to mention her desecration at the hands of the Dadaists and the Surrealists. According to Vasari, she was a young Florentine, Monna Lisa, who in 1495 married the successful silk merchant Francesco del Giocondo; hence the painting's appellation in Italian, *La Gioconda*. It is probable that the work dates to between 1503 and 1505; that is, to Leonardo's second Florentine period. Leonardo was extremely fond of this painting, to the point of carrying it with him to France where it was finally sold to Francis I, either by Leonardo himself or by Melzi. Greatly admired and always considered the prototype Rennaisance portrait, the *Mona Lisa* acquired even greater renown when it was stolen in 1911 from the Salon Carré by a house-painter, Vincenzo Peruggia. It was found in a hotel in Florence two years later.

The entire painting is suffused with an infinite sweetness and gentility. One of Leonardo's techniques for achieving this incomparable result was the sfumato, a slow, progressive blurring, near-disintegration of the forms, a continual blending of light and shadow.

Madonna and Child in Majesty Surrounded by Angels by Cimabue (ca. 1240 to after 1302), probably painted for the church of San Francesco in Pisa, where it was found in 1813 and moved to the Louvre. The painting reveals much about Cimabue's rapport with the monumental sculpture of Nicola Pisano in the years preceding 1272. This panel is exemplary of a fundamental characteristic of Cimabue's art, that precise, incisive drawing and powerful chiaroscuro that together create a strong sense of plasticity.

In the **Battle of San Romano**, Paolo Uccello (1397-1475) evokes one of the culminating moments of the clash that in June of 1432 pitted the Florentines led by Niccolò Mauruzi da Tolentino against the forces of Siena under Bernardino della Ciarda, at San Romano. We know that Paolo Uccello represented three episodes of the battle in the same number of panels, now in the Louvre, the National Gallery of London, and the Galleria degli Uffizi in Florence. This painting in the Louvre illustrates the action by Micheletto da Cotignola on the Florentine flank. The leader is shown at the center of the composition amid horses spurred on to the attack; above the geometrical armor and the elaborate helms, a forest of cavalry lances.

Painted in a 6-year period (1451 to 1457) for Palazzo Medici in Florence, this panel is the best preserved of the three, to the point that the silver of the armor is still clearly distinguishable.

Saint Sebastian
by Andrea Mantegna (1431-1506).
This canvas was recorded as being in a small town in central France, where it remained until 1910. Mantegna composed this monumental work using heavy masses, demonstrating his understanding of both Roman architecture and the prospective vision of the Florentines.
The saint's heroic acceptance of martyrdom offsets the coldly "archaeological" quality of the composition as a whole.

patriotic, and musical events and industrial expositions, an examination hall, and finally, a venue for temporary exhibits. The museum is now home to an exceptional collection, counting 144 masterpieces of post-Impressionist painting. The nucleus of the collection was amassed by Paul Guillaume. After Guillaume's death, his widow Domenica married tycoon Jean Walter and united her husbands' collections, which she donated to the French government, requesting upon transfer that the corpus of paintings remain intact. The museum exhibits works by Soutine, Cézanne, Picasso, Van Dongen, and Modigliani. In 1927, Claude Monet's *Water Lilies* were hung in the two oval ground-floor halls. Following restoration work that lasted for six years, the museum reopened in 2006. The work included considerable architectural alterations that now permit naturally illuminating the spaces housing Monet's masterpieces.

Orangerie

As the name suggests, this museum is installed in what was once an orange-house, built in 1852 to shelter the Tuileries' orange trees during the winter. It was a long building with the glassed-in side opening on the Seine and the blind side on the garden. At the time of the Third Republic it was used for various purposes: a multifunctional hall hosting sports,

Monet's *Water Lilies*

In March 1883, Claude Monet rented a house in Giverny, Eure, at the confluence of the Seine and the Epte, and moved there with his family. He installed a magnificent garden and built a boathouse, which he used for painting on the water. His pond was also adorned with a small hog-backed bridge and numerous weeping willows and exotic plants along the banks: Monet had recreated what was almost a corner of Japan in Giverny, a reflection of that taste and passion for Japanese culture that began to spread throughout Europe in about 1870, sparked by the publication of Japanese floral prints. This is the pool in which the painter cultivated those water lilies he painted in his large boathouse atelier for about 20 years, even when his cataracts had made him almost blind.

Cézanne affirmed that no one, before Monet, had so sublimely represented water and its myriad reflections. And in fact, for years and years Monet concentrated on the surface of the pool, observing it at all hours of the day, from the first light of dawn to twilight and at night, studying the reflections, the color changes, the most subtle nuances. He was completely absorbed in this study, and wrote to the art dealer Durand-Ruel: "These landscapes of water and reflections have become an obsession for me. It is beyond my strength as an old man, and yet I so want to render what I feel."

In these *Water Lilies*, the subject fills the entire surface of the canvas; for each painting, Monet selected a precise palette, from the softest, lightest yellows and greens to the very deepest indigoes, from the most diaphanous of pinks to the most intense blues.

The art critic André Masson speaks of these works as embodying a "cosmic vision" in which the surface of the water is transformed into the entire universe. He defined the Orangerie as the "Sistine Chapel of Impressionism."

Place du Carrousel

This plaza occupies the site on which the Tuileries Palace stood before it burned down in 1871. The entrance portal is all that remains today of this magnificent palace. In 1964-1965, a sort of open-air museum was organized here to display works of sculpture. The most important include works by Aristide Maillol such as *Night* and *Reclining Woman*.

ARC DU CARROUSEL – Designed by Pierre-François Fontaine and Charles Percier, the arch was built between 1806 and 1808 to celebrate the victories of Napoleon Bonaparte in 1805. It imitates both the architectural design and the decoration of the Arch of Septimius Severus in Rome. Red and white marble columns frame the three archways; bas-reliefs on all the faces recall the emperor's victories. On top of it were placed the four gilded horses which had been removed by order of Napoleon from the Venetian Basilica of San Marco, to which they were returned in 1815. The originals were replaced by copies; the chariot with the statue of Peace, led by gilded Victories, was added later.

The Arc du Carrousel, with in the far background the obelisk in Place de la Concorde; right, a detail of the quadriga on the summit of the arch.

Jardin des Tuileries

The Tuileries garden extends for about one kilometer from Place du Carrousel to Place de la Concorde. The land was purchased by Catherine de' Medici in 1563 for installing an English pleasure garden, which was refurbished by Le Nôtre in 1663. The pilasters of the majestic entrance gate are flanked by statues of *Mercury* and *Fame*, both riding Pegasus, by Coysevox.

Images of the Jardin des Tuileries, dotted with statuary groups, overflowing vases and plant pots, and elegant lamp posts. Although redesigned several times, the garden still follows Le Nôtre's original layout.

Place de la Concorde

Created between 1757 and 1779 to a design by Jacques-Ange Gabriel on land donated by the king in 1743, the square was originally dedicated to Louis XV. An equestrian statue of the king, a work by Bouchardon and Pigalle, stood in the center but was pulled down during the French Revolution. During the Revolution, this became the site of the guillotine, under whose blade so many great figures of the time lost their heads: from the king, Louis XVI, and his queen, Marie-Antoinette, to Madame Roland and Robespierre. The square became Place de la Concorde in 1795, and its present-day appearance dates from work supervised by the architect Hittorf between 1836 and 1840. In the center of the square stands the Egyptian obelisk from the temple of Luxor, donated to Louis-Philippe in 1831 by Mehmet-Ali. Erected in 1836, it is 23 meters high and covered with hieroglyphics illustrating the glorious deeds of the pharaoh Ramses II. Eight statues, symbolizing the main cities of France, stand at the corners of the square. To the north of the square, on either side of Rue Royale, are the colonnaded buildings (these too designed by Gabriel) of the Ministry of the Navy and the Hôtel Crillon.

Views of Place de la Concorde, with the obelisk of Ramses II rising in counterpoint to the Tour Eiffel in the background. The imaginative lamp posts greatly enrich the unique urban furnishings of this plaza.

Fountains in Place de la Concorde
Built on the model of the fountains in St. Peter's Square in Rome, these two fountains at the sides of the obelisk were erected by Hittorf between 1836 and 1846; they have several basins and the statues adorning them are allegories of rivers. There are perhaps few places in the world with the magical atmosphere of enchantment present at every hour of the day in this square. At night, under the light of the street lamps, the ambiance becomes unreal, almost fable-like.

Pont Alexandre III

At the end of Avenue Winston Churchill, Pont Alexandre III unites the Esplanade des Invalides and the Champs-Elysées with a single metal span, 107 meters in length and 40 in width. Built in the years 1896 to 1900, the bridge is named for Czar Alexander III, whose son Nicholas II inaugurated it as part of the celebrations for the Russo-French alliance.

Flowered garlands, extravagant lamps supported by cherubs, allegories in the form of water-sprites and spirits make up the rich decoration that embellishes the bridge. On the two Rive Droite pylons are representations of Medieval France and Modern France, while the Rive Gauche side is adorned with statues representing Renaissance France and the France of Louis XIV. Allegories of the Seine and the Neva, again symbols of France and Russia, tower over the pylons at the centers of the bridge entrance arches.

Pont Alexandre III and some details of its rich decoration.

Musée d'Orsay

What the press has defined as "the most beautiful museum in Europe" is found on the left bank of the Seine where the State Audit Court, destroyed in 1870 during the Commune, originally stood. In 1898, the Paris-Orléans railway company assigned construction of the new station to Victor Laloux. The work was carried out in two years so that the Gare d'Orsay would be ready for the 1900 Universal Exposition. Laloux designed a grandiose nave, 135 by 40 meters, the metal structure of which was skilfully covered on the outside by light-coloured stucco work. The interior not only housed the sixteen platforms but also restaurants and an elegant hotel with at least 400 rooms. Abandoned in 1939, the Gare d'Orsay went into a slow decline under the specter of demolition: Orson Welles's cultural revival with the filming of *The Trial* and establishment of Jean-Louis Barrault's company there were of no avail. In 1973, French President Georges Pompidou declared it a national monument and launched the project that converted it to a museum displaying the half century of art, from Napoleon III's Second Empire to early Cubism. It proved to be a perfect link between the Louvre, a temple of ancient art, and the Centre Georges Pompidou, a temple of modern art. Tender for contract for its restructuring commenced in 1978 and was won by the ACT group; the Italian architect Gae Aulenti was entrusted with the inte-

The museum seen from the Seine and a comprehensive view of the beautiful interior, with the original glass roof and the coffered ceiling.

rior decorating. Nowadays more than 4000 works, including paintings, sculptures, drawings, and furniture, are exhibited in over 45,000 square meters.
The ground-floor collections of painting, sculpture, and the decorative arts from 1850 to 1870 feature works by Ingres, Delacroix, Manet, Puvis de Chavannes, and Gustave Moreau.

Vincent Van Gogh (1853-1890) – Portrait of Dr. Gachet.
Painted in Auvers-sur-Oise, this work portrays Dr. Paul Gachet leaning on a red table; he is "very fair, very light," as the painter wrote to his brother Theo, with his "grief-hardened face" set in "the heartbroken expression of our times."

Vincent Van Gogh (1853-1890) – The Church at Auvers and **Self-Portrait** (top left and center) and **Bedroom in Arles** (bottom). The latter two canvases were painted in Provence in 1889, while *The Church at Auvers* dates to the very last days of the life of the painter, who committed suicide in the fields near the church on 28 July 1890. Top right, **The Toilette by Henri de Toulouse-Lautrec (1864-1901)**.

Impressionist paintings (Monet, Renoir, Pissarro, Degas, and Manet), the Personnaz, Gachet, and Guillaumin Collections, and Post-Impressionist paintings, with masterpieces by Seurat, Signac, Toulouse-Lautrec, Gauguin, Van Gogh, and the Nabis group (Bonnard, Vuillard, and Vallotton), are displayed on the top floor. Lastly, the middle floor features art from 1870 to 1914: the official art of the Third Republic, Symbolism, academic painting, and the decorative arts of the Art Nouveau period, with Guimard, Emile Gallé, and the School of Nancy.

Gustave Moreau (1826-1898) – Jason and Medea.
The art of Gustave Moreau, jewel-like and refined, has many points of contact with Symbolist poetry in the richness of detail, the complexity of vision, the atmosphere of mysticism that pervades all his production. This painting triumphed at the 1865 Salon thanks to its magical atmosphere made of bright colors and sensual notes. Note the citations of Leonardo's *Virgin of the Rocks* in the background landscape on the left, and the pose of Medea, which is analogous in many ways to that of *Leda*.

Jean-Auguste Ingres (1780-1867) – The Spring.
When he painted *The Spring*, Ingres was already a celebrated artist and had opened an atelier. His many students adored him, despite his dreadful character and his execrable manners. A pupil of David, Ingres pushed the arabesque of the outline, the undulating line, to its apogee. *The Spring*, completed in 1856, is one of Ingres' last works and the best-known example of that "soft" style of painting dominated by sinuous forms that was to be carried forward by his pupils Hippolyte Flandrin and Eugène Amauray-Duval. This splendid female nude was universally received with great enthusiasm; here the body, in the same sinuous line that had earlier defined odalisques and bathers, attains absolute harmony and perfection.

Edgar Degas (1834-1917) – The Bellelli Family. Begun in 1858 during a stay in Florence, this painting has a simple, severe compositive impact, based on the interplay of blacks and whites and enriched by the perspective created by the reflection in the mirror above the hearth.

Auguste Renoir (1841-1919) – The Moulin de la Gallette. A masterpiece of Impressionist painting, this carefree open-air dance is shot with patches of light that create a sensation of lively movement on a Montmartre Sunday.

Edouard Manet (1832-1883) – The Luncheon on the Grass. Painted in 1863 and rejected by the Salon because it was deemed scandalous, the painting is inspired by antique art in the painter's choice of a classical subject: think only of Venetian painting and Titian's *Concert Champêtre*. The subject, judged immoral and provocative, and the brutality and immediacy of the style made Manet a "primitive" of a new era in painting. The light, filtered by the leaves, illuminates the figures gathered in the coolness of a glade, with a technique as revolutionary as the content.

Edouard Manet (1832-1883) – Olympia. With this canvas, painted in 1863, Manet broke totally with tradition, destroying volume, abolishing intermediate hues and half tones, and relying solely on free juxtaposition of luminous colors. *Olympia*, presented at the Salon of 1865, scandalized the public and official criticism and was contemptuously defined the "yellow-bellied odalisque."

Claude Monet (1840-1926) – Women in the Garden. Painted in 1867 at Ville d'Avray "en plein air," this canvas reveals the depth of Monet's research into light. Sunlight falls straight down on the flowered garden, while the whole compositions seems to be cut in two by shadow and light.

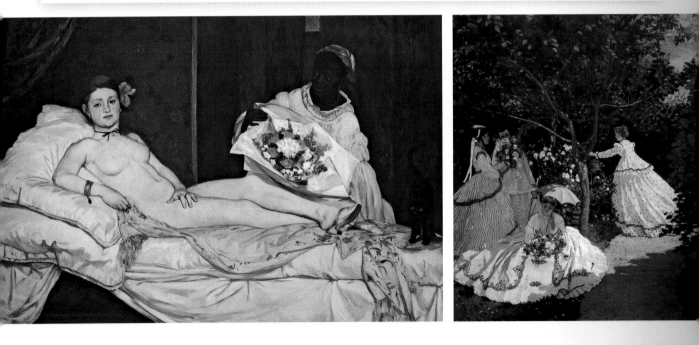

Paul Cézanne (1839-1906) – Apples and Oranges; Card Players.
Dubbed the "solidifier of Impressionism," Cézanne indeed expresses great solidity and depth of perspective in these two canvases.

Henri de Toulouse-Lautrec (1864-1901) – The Lady Clown Cha-U-Kao.
The world of the Moulin Rouge revisited by the artist in the gentle, resigned humanity of one of its pathetic characters.

Claude Monet (1840-1926) – Rouen Cathedral.
By representing the same subject over and over as it was transformed by the passing of the hours, Monet produced more than twenty canvases of the cathedral of Rouen.

Paul Gauguin (1848-1903) – Arearea; Tahitian Women (On the Beach). Two scenes of great serenity and peace, in which Gauguin discovers primitive art with its heavy, flat forms and the bright and violent colors of untamed nature. Painting by painting, Gauguin moved away from Impressionism toward a more solid, more highly-contrasted style.

Henri Rousseau (1844-1910) – The Snake Charmer.

Grand Palais

Built for the 1900 Universal Exposition to plans by the architects Henri Deglane, Louis Louvet, Albert Thomas, and Charles Girault, the Grand Palais is a marvelous example of Art Nouveau style. Its facade, 240 meters in length and rising to 20 meters, is marked off by Ionic columns in a broad colonnade and decorated with friezes and sculptural compositions. The building is now the home of the Palais de le Découverte, dedicated to the sciences and their applications, a planetarium, the Galeries Nationales du Grand Palais, which since 1964 are venues for international art exhibits, and the huge, magnificent central nave that hosts various cultural events. Following recent restoration, the Grand Palais reopened in 2005: on that occasion, the two famous globes created by Vincenzo Coronelli in 1681-1683 for Louis XIV, masterpieces of Baroque cartography, were placed on exhibit.

Petit Palais

Built by Charles Girault for the 1900 Universal Exposition in an eclectic style typical of the late 19th century, the palace consists of a monumental portico crowned by a dome and flanked by two colonnades. At present, it contains the collection of the City of Paris with countless 19th-century paintings and sculptures and the Tuck and Dutuit collections.

The magnificent, formal facades of the Grand Palais (left) and the Petit Palais (bottom).

The corners of the Grand Palais are crowned by enormous, imperious **quadrigae** of such plasticism that they almost seem to attempt to leap out of the curves of the facade to gallop freely in the air. By Georges Récipon, they represent *Harmony Triumphing over Discord* (on the Seine side) and *Immortality Trumping Time* (facing the Champs-Elysées).

Champs-Elysées

Originally, this vast area lying to the west of Place de la Concorde was swamp land. After its reclamation, Le Nôtre in 1667 designed the wide avenue called Grand-Cours (which became the Champs-Elysées in 1709), reaching from the Tuileries as far as Place de l'Etoile, today called Place De Gaulle. At the time of the Second Empire, this became the most fashionable meeting-place and upper-class residential area in all Paris. Today it may no longer have its one-time aristocratic character, but it has lost nothing of its beauty and elegance: luxurious shops, theaters, famous restaurants, and important airline offices line the boulevard, which is always full of Parisians, tourists, and a cosmopolitan throng.

Two suggestive aerial views of what has been defined "the world's most beautiful boulevard." About halfway along its length it is broken by the Rond-Point des Champs-Elysées, an important traffic circle, 140 meters in diameter, designed by Le Nôtre.

Arc de Triomphe

At the end of the Champs-Elysées, at the top of the Chaillot hill, is the large Place De Gaulle; radiating outwards from this square are no less than twelve main arteries. Isolated in the center stands the powerful and imposing Arch of Triumph, begun by Chalgrin in 1806 under Napoleon I, who ordered it as a memorial to the Grande Armée. Completed in 1836, it has a single barrel-vault and actually exceeds in size the Arch of Constantine in Rome: in fact it is 50 meters high and 45 meters wide. The faces of the arch have huge bas-reliefs, of which the best known and finest piece is that on the right, on the part of the arch facing the Champs-Elysées, depicting the departure of the volunteers in 1792 and called the *Marseillaise*. The principal victories of Napoleon are celebrated in the other bas-reliefs higher up, while the shields sculpted in the top section bear the names of the great battles.

The Arc de Triomphe today and as it looked in the early 20th century, in a painting by Georges Stein (Musée Carnavalet).

The tomb of the unknown soldier was placed under the arch in 1920 and its eternal flame is tended every evening. There is a history of the monument in a small museum inside the arch, where one can read the names of no less than 558 generals, some of them underlined because they died on the battlefield.

Tour Eiffel

Erected on occasion of the Paris Universal Exposition of 1889, the tower bears mute testimony to man's innate will to create things that attest to the measure of his genius. Those were the years of the Industrial Revolution, years lived under the banner of progress, of scientific conquest, and architecture like everything else underwent radical changes: glass, iron, and steel were the new construction materials that made any building lighter, more dynamic, more modern. The engineer replaced the architect. And it was in fact an engineer, Gustave Eiffel, who designed no longer on paper, but in the sky this extraordinary metal spear that seems to triumph over all the city's ancient monuments. A total of 320 meters in height, the tower is a light welded interweave of 15,000 separate pieces of metal. It weighs seven thousand tons and rests on four enormous pylons with concrete bases. The tower has three floors: the first at 57 meters, the second at 115, and the third at 274. On the first two floors, the tourist will find restaurants and bars that are perfect for taking a break and admiring utterly unique views of the city. On the first floor, the name of the "Altitude 95" restaurant reminds us just how high we are above sea level. The second floor is instead accessible by private elevator to one of France's top restaurants, the "Jules Verne," with view of the bridges of Paris and the city itself and its sophisticated decor styled by Loup and Slavik.

Several images of the monument that Parisians have always called "the Iron Lady" (La Dame de Fer). Construction began on 1 July 1887 and the tower was inaugurated on 15 May 1889.

The Tour Eiffel in Numbers

15 May 1889: day of the inauguration

22 months: duration of construction

1710 steps to the top

150 workers

50 engineers

40 designers

700 engineering drawings

120 million visitors in 100 years.

And yet, Paris' welcome to the tower at its opening was not unanimous. Some people felt it was appalling: 47 "opinion makers," including Guy de Maupassant, Alexandre Dumas, Charles Gounod, Victorien Sardou, and Charles Garnier, who defined themselves as "lovers of the beauty of Paris," protested vociferously against the "useless and monstrous Eiffel Tower ... which even commercial America refuses ...."

A meeting-place and a must as a milieu for a stroll when visiting Paris, the **Jardins du Trocadéro** extend over 93,000 square meters on the Chaillot hill and offer one of the best views anywhere of the Tour Eiffel, which rises exactly opposite. At the center is a large pool, from which the waters descend toward the Pont d'Iéna in a series of cascades, jets, sprays, and vertical fountains throwing more than 8000 cubic meters of water into the air every hour (the Fontaine de Varsovie, 1937).

Palais de Chaillot

Along with the Trocadéro gardens, the Champs-Elysées, and the Eiffel Tower, the Palais de Chaillot constitutes a fine example of early 20th-century architecture. It was built for the Universal Exposition held in Paris in 1937. Its architects were Boileau, Azéma, and Carlu, who planned the present building on the site of previous structure, the Trocadéro, so-called to commemorate the taking of the fortress at Trocadero, Spain, which defended the port of Cádiz, by the duke of Angoulême on 31 August 1823.

The Chaillot Palace consists of two enormous pavilions which stretch out in two wings, united by a central terrace with statues of gilt bronze. The two pavilions, on the front of which are engraved verses by the poet Valéry, today contain the Musée National de la Marine, the Musée de l'Homme, and the Musée des Monuments Français.

The Jardins du Trocadéro are adorned with a lot of sculptures, many of which date to the 1930s. One very interesting piece is the gilded bronze, by Paul Jouve, of a fighting bull.

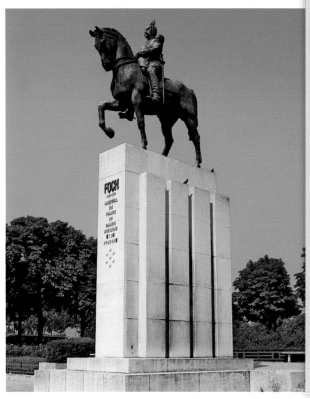

Musée National de la Marine – This is one of the richest naval museums in the world. It contains models of ships, original objects, mementos, and works of art linked to the sea. Among these are the model of Columbus' ship the *Santa Maria* and the ship *La Belle Poule*, which brought the ashes of Napoleon back to France from St. Helena.

Musée de l'Homme – The Museum of Man contains important anthropological and ethnological collections illustrating the various human races and their ways of life. The gallery of paleontology exhibits some very famous prehistoric discoveries: the Lespugue *Venus*, made from mammoth ivory, a cast of the Hottentot *Venus*, and the *Hoggar frescoes*.

Musée des Monuments Français – Born in 1880 from an idea of Viollet-le-Duc, the Museum of French Monuments offers a vast artistic panorama from the Carolingian period on. The works are grouped according to regions, schools, and periods, so that the visitor can study the evolution, characteristics, and influence of each style. Also in the Palais de Chaillot complex is the **Théâtre de Chaillot**, situated below the terrace, with a capacity of 3000. In 1948 and in 1951-1952 it was used for the third and sixth sessions of the General Assembly of the United Nations. In a grotto in the garden is the **Aquarium**, home to exemplars of most of France's freshwater fish species. The gardens slope gently down to the Seine to the **Pont d'Iéna** (1813) crossing. Adorned with four equestrian groups at the ends, the bridge links Place de Varsovie to the other bank, dominated by the Eiffel Tower.

Champ-de-Mars

The green carpet stretching out from the Tour Eiffel was originally a military parade ground that was later transformed into a park. Festivals were held here during the Ancien Régime and the Revolution, one of the most famous was the Fête de l'Être Suprême introduced by Robespierre and celebrated on 8 June 1794; the tradition continued into modern times with various Universal Expositions. Today's park area, laid out by Formigé in

The broad green expanse of the Champ-de-Mars seen from the top of the Tour Eiffel.

1908-1928, is crossed by wide boulevards and boasts small lakes, watercourses, and a profusion of flowerbeds.

Ecole Militaire

This building, at the south end of the Champ-de-Mars, is the result of an initiative by the financier Pâris-Duverny and Madame Pompadour designed to permit men of the poorer classes to take up military careers. The Ecole Royale Militaire was built in 1751-1773 to plans by Jacques-Ange Gabriel, in a sober style with harmonious lines. The facade has two orders of windows; the columns of the pavilion at the center support the pediment, which is decorated with statues and covered by a cupola. At the rear, on the Place de Fontenay side, is the elegant Courtyard of Honor with a portico of twinned Doric columns and facade composed of three pavilions linked by two rows of columns. The building is still the seat of a military school. In 1784, Napoleon Bonaparte was admitted to the school, where he completed the two-year course in artillery in a single year. Upon graduation he was commissioned a second lieutenant.

Musée du Quai Branly

The Musée du Quai Branly, designed by Jean Nouvel, boasts an extraordinary setting on the banks of the Seine, almost hidden by dense plantings (Patrick Blanc's "vertical gardens" or *mur vegetal*), protected from the Seine embankment traffic by an enormous decorated curved glass wall, again by Jean Nouvel. With this museum, the art of Africa, Oceania, Asia, and the Americas has won a place in the heart of the city's great historic-artistic circuit. Particular attention is dedicated to the historical aspects of the cultures that are presented, the different meanings of the various works, and some important thematic explanations. Two listening and projection rooms aid the visitor in correctly placing the works in their contexts. Inside the museum you'll also find the Tour Musique, a large glass tower on five levels displaying 8700 musical instruments.

Alongside the rooms exhibiting the permanent collections and the spaces for temporary exhibits, the complex also features spaces reserved for researchers, a mediathèque, an auditorium, and several conference and meeting rooms.

Bottom, an overall view of the Musée du Quai Branly; right, an anthropomorphic African mask from Benin, on display in the museum.

Les Invalides

Stretching between Place Vauban and the Esplanade des Invalides, this vast complex of buildings includes the Hôtel des Invalides, the Dôme, and the church of St. Louis. The whole construction, ordered by Louis XIV and entrusted to

Libéral Bruant in 1671, was built to house old and invalid soldiers who were then often forced to beg for a living. The vast square of the Esplanade, 487 meters long and 250 meters wide, designed between 1704 and 1720, creates a perfect surround for the Hôtel des Invalides. In the garden in front of the Hôtel are a line of bronze cannon from the 17th and 18th centuries, eighteen pieces that form the "triumphal battery" fired only on important occasions; at the sides of the entrance are two German tanks captured in 1944. The severe facade, 196 meters long, has four orders of windows and a majestic portal in the center, surmounted by a relief representing Louis XIV with Prudence and Justice at his sides. The four sides of the courtyard are regular in form, each with two stories of arcades. The pavilion at the end thus becomes the facade of the church of St. Louis. In the center is a statue of Napoleon by Seurre. Worth seeing, inside the church of St-Louis-des-Invalides, is the Chapel of Napoleon, which houses the hearse in which the remains of the emperor were taken to St. Helena for burial and the sarcophagus in which Napoleon's body was brought back to France in 1840.

Dôme des Invalides

Considered one of the architect Hardouin-Mansart's masterpieces, the Dôme was erected between 1679 and 1706. Pure forms and a classical, sober style distinguish this building, with its square plan and two orders. The facade is a work of elegance and symmetry: above the two orders of columns surmounted by a pediment is the solid mass of the drum with its twin columns; above, from a restrained series of corbels,

The facade and entrance to the Hôtel des Invalides and, right, the regal architecture of the Dôme.

A porphyry sarcophagus, watched over by twelve statues of Victory, holds the remains of Napoleon in the crypt of the Dôme des Invalides.

springs the slim cupola with its decorations of flower garlands and other floral motifs. The gilded leaves that decorate the top shine in the sunlight, and the structure terminates with a small lantern with spire 107 meters above ground level. The interior, in the form of a Greek cross, reflects the simplicity characteristic of the exterior. In the pendentives of the dome, Charles de la Fosse painted the four Evangelists, while in the center he depicted the figure of St. Louis offering Christ the sword with which he defeated the infidels. Directly under the dome is the entrance to the crypt containing the tomb of Napoleon; indeed, the entire church could be said to be a shrine to the memory of Napoleon. Here too are tombs of members of the emperor's family as well as those of other great Frenchmen. In the chapels on the right are the tombs of Napoleon's brother, Joseph Bonaparte, and of the marshals Vauban and Foch. The emperor's other brother, Jérôme, is buried in the first chapel on the left.

Tomb of Napoleon I

Napoleon Bonaparte died on 5 May 1821 on St. Helena, but not until many years later were the French able to obtain permission from England to bring back the remains of their emperor to his own country. Louis-Philippe sent his son, the prince of Joinville, to St. Helena to supervise the exhumation of the emperor's body. The re-entry into France was the last triumphal voyage of the Frenchman best loved by his people, most venerated by his soldiers, and most feared by his enemies. In September 1840 a French ship carried the body of Napoleon to Le Havre, then slowly made the trip up the Seine as far as Paris. On 15 December, in a snowstorm, almost the entire city attended the funeral of the emperor, whose body moved in a slow procession along the great boulevards, passing under the Arc de Triomphe and descending the Champs-Elysées to come to rest in the Dôme des Invalides and thus end at last Napoleon's long exile. Like those of an Egyptian pharaoh, the remains were contained in six coffins: the first of tin, the second of mahogany, the third and fourth of lead, the fifth of ebony, and the sixth of oak. These were then placed in the huge sarcophagus of red granite, in the crypt specially designed for the purpose by the great architect Visconti. Here 12 enormous Victories, the work of Pradier, keep a vigil over the emperor, as if to symbolise the whole French people, finally reunited with their great hero. And as if to unite him after death with one from whom he had been divided during his life, next to the tomb was placed the tomb of Napoleon's son, the King of Rome, known romantically as "l'Aiglon" (the "Eaglet").

Dôme des Invalides

Since the end of the First Empire, a true necropolis has taken form in the shadow of the Dôme des Invalides. This is the final resting place of France's greatest military leaders, including, besides the son and brothers of Napoleon:

Henri de la Tour d'Auvergne (Marshal General Turenne)

The heart of Sebastien de Vauban, designer of Louis XIV's military fortifications

The heart of General Charles Leclerc, Napoleon's brother-in-law

The heart of Théophile Malo de la Tour d'Auvergne

General Duroc, Grand Marshal of the Palace for Napoleon

General Bertrand, Grand Marshal of the Palace for Napoleon

The ashes of General Marceau

The heart of General Kléber

Marshal Lyautey

Marshal Foch

General Nivelle

General Mangin

Rouget de Lisle, composer of *La Marseillaise*

Marshal de Mac-Mahon

Marshal Leclerc de Hauteclocque

Marshal Juin

The 14 victims of the Fieschi attentat of 28 July 1835

Tomb of Napoleon I, in Finnish red porphyry. Since 1940, Napoleon's only legitimate son, Napoleon II, who died of tuberculosis in Vienna at just 21 years of age, in 1832, rests in a niche in the crypt of Napoleon.

In the chapels, the tombs of Napoleon's closest relatives, including his two brothers, Joseph King of Spain and Jérôme King of Westphalia, with the heart of the latter's wife, the Princess of Württemberg, and the couple's son Napoléon-Joseph-Charles-Paul, also called Prince Napoléon Jérôme.

Palais Bourbon

This building bears the signature of no less than four famous architects: Giardini began it in 1722, Lassurance continued its construction, and Aubert and Gabriel completed it in 1728. It was originally built for the daughter of Louis XIV, the Duchess of Bourbon, who gave her name to the building. In 1764 it became the property of the Condé prince, who had it extended to its present dimensions, an imposing and noble structure looking over the square of the same name. The portico of the facade has an allegorical pediment sculpted by Cortot in 1842. Other allegorical bas-reliefs on the wings are by Rude and Pradier. The interior has a wealth of works of art: suffice it to say that between 1838 and 1845 Delacroix decorated its library with the History of Civilization and in the same room are busts of Diderot and Voltaire sculpted by Houdon. Once the seat of the Council of the Five Hundred and then of the Chamber of Deputies, the building is now the meeting-place of the French National Assembly.

The grand and elegant facade of the Palais Bourbon, today the seat of the French National Assembly.

Palais du Luxembourg

On the death of Henry IV, his queen, Marie de' Medici, who apparently did not feel at home in the Louvre, preferred to live in a place which in some way reminded her of Florence, the city from which she came. Thus in 1612 she acquired this mansion from Duke François de Luxembourg, together with a considerable expanse of ground, and in 1615 she commissioned Salomon de Brosse to build a palace as near as possible in style and materials to the Florentine palaces she had left behind. And in fact both the rusticated stonework and the large columns and rings are much more reminiscent of the Palazzo Pitti in Florence than of any Parisian building. The facade consists of a pavilion with two orders covered by a cupola, with two pavilions at the sides, united to the central unit by galleries. When the Revolution broke out, the palace was taken from the royal family and transformed into a state prison.

On 4 November 1795, the first Directory installed itself here, and later Napoleon decided that it would be the seat of the Senate.

For more than a generation, the gardens of the Palais du Luxembourg have been Paris' most popular. The adjacent Petit Luxembourg palace is the official residence of the president of the Senate.

Jardins du Luxembourg

Perhaps one of the most pleasant and typical things about Paris, this city with so many different aspects, is that along with roads crowded with traffic, people, and noise there are hidden corners of greenery and silence, oases of peace where time slows to a stop.

The Jardins du Luxembourg extend over 23 hectares: they were redesigned in the 19th century by Chalgrin, who despite alterations remained substantially faithful to Marie de' Medici's original plans. Among the trees, throughout its vast area, are such attractions as fountains, groups of statues, a Grand Guignol puppet theater, and a merry-go-round designed by Garnier. A fine series of statues portray the queens of France and other illustrious women along the terraces of the park.

The decoration in the Jardins du Luxembourg is extremely varied, comprising both classical statuary, by Carpeaux, and works of contemporary art, many of which are amusing and fanciful.

Medici Fountain

At the end of a canal on the eastern side of the Palais du Luxembourg, in a lush green setting, is the splendid Medici Fountain attributed to Salomon de Brosse. In the central niche, Polyphemus is depicted as he surprises Galatea with the shepherd Acis, a work by Ottin (1863), while on the back is a bas-relief by Valois dating from 1806 and depicting Leda and the Swan.

Observatory Fountain

The route from the Jardins du Luxembourg to Observatory leads along the magnificent tree-lined Avenue de l'Observatoire. And here, in a setting of lush green, is the Observatory Fountain, created by Davioud in 1875 and known for its sculptural decoration, by Carpeaux, representing the four quarters of the globe as four unusually beautiful and graceful female figures supporting the massive orb of the earth.

The Medici Fountain, right, and the Observatory Fountain, bottom.

Panthéon

Born as the church of Sainte-Geneviève in fulfilment of a vow made by Louis XV during a serious illness in 1744, the Panthéon, designed by Soufflot, was begun in 1758 and completed with the contribution of Rondelet in 1789. During the Revolution it became the Temple of Glory, used for the burial of great men. Soufflot sought a decidedly classical style, a return to the ancient world. Its dimensions, first of all, are exceptional: 110 meters long by 83 meters high. A stairway in front of the temple leads up to a pronaos with 22 columns, which support a pediment on which in 1831 David d'Angers sculpted the allegorical work representing the Fatherland between Liberty and History. Here one can also read the famous inscription: *Aux grands hommes, la patrie reconnaissante* ("To the great men, from their grateful fatherland"). The whole building is dominated by the great cupola, similar to Christopher Wren's dome on the church of St. Paul in London; here too, the drum is surrounded by a ring of Corinthian columns. The interior is in the form of a Greek cross, with the cupola above the crossing, supported by four piers, on one of which is the tomb of Rousseau. The walls are decorated with paintings: the most famous are those by Puvis de Chavannes, illustrating stories of St. Geneviève. The crypt below the temple contains many tombs of illustrious men. Worth recalling are those of Victor Hugo (brought here in 1885), Emile Zola, Voltaire, the designer Soufflot himself, Carnot, and Mirabeau.

The majestic Panthéon building. In the interior is the unusual tomb of Jean-Jacques Rousseau (left), among others.

Foucault's Pendulum

The Panthéon houses a singular instrument designed to experimentally demonstrate the astronomical phenomenon of the Earth's rotation on its axis. This gigantic pendulum owes its name to the French physicist Jean Bernard Léon Foucault, whose fundamental— yet totally fortuitous—intuition took this monumental form on occasion of the International Exposition of 1851. A few weeks later, with a 67-meter wire, Foucault suspended a 28-kg brass sphere from the dome of the Panthéon in such a manner as to leave it free to swing in any direction for many hours. The idea was that in order to demonstrate the rotation of the Earth it would be necessary to set up an object that would remain stationary while the Earth turned beneath it. And this was the first Foucault pendulum: presented to an admiring public, it showed, with its pointer that grazed the sand-covered floor, that its plane of oscillation tended to rotate slowly. Since once made to oscillate, a body always oscillates in the same plane (in other words, the plane of oscillation of a pendulum remains fixed in space), if the Earth were stationary the pointer should always have traced and retraced the same line. Instead, the marks left in the sand showed that the floor (hence the ground) was rotating with respect to the plane in which the pendulum was oscillating. The lines drawn by the pointer changed direction slowly, and after 24 hours once again coincided with the original incision.

Many other pendula of this type have been installed in many parts of the world. And in the fall of 1995, Foucault's original pendulum once again took up its march under the dome of the Paris Panthéon.

Paintings and Sculptures in the Panthéon

Sainte Geneviève
watching over Paris

The Apotheosis of Sainte Geneviève

Monument to the generals
of the Revolution

Monument to
the orators and
propagandists
of the Restoration

Saint Geneviève meeting
Saint Germain

Monument to
Diderot and the
Encyclopaedists

West Pediment
The allegory of France distributes laurels to great men
of civil and military history. The crowns are proffered
by Liberty, while Glory inscribes their names

The meeting
of Saint Germain
and Geneviève
in her childhood

AUX GRANDS HOMMES LA PATRIE RECONNAISSANTE

The National Convention monument

The baptism of Clovis

The coronation of Charlemagne

Foucault's Pendulum

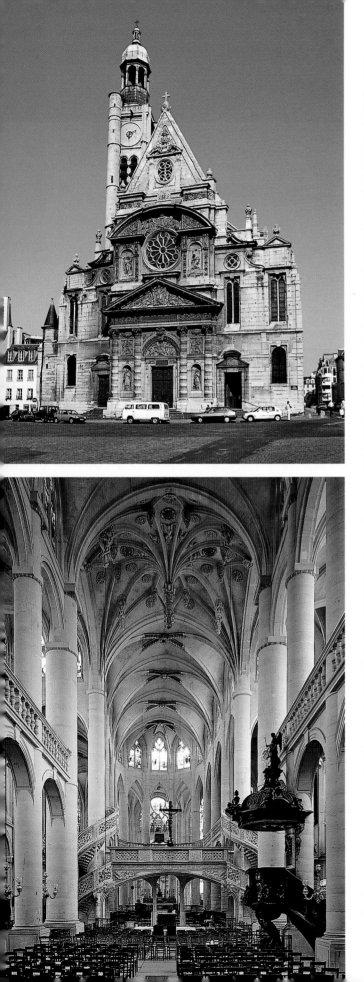

St-Etienne-du-Mont

This church, one of the most remarkable in Paris both for its facade and for the interior, stands in the city's most picturesque zone, the Latin Quarter. The University of Paris first appeared in the area in the late 13th century and immediately became famous throughout the world of Western culture because of the names of the great masters who gave lessons there: St. Bonaventura and St. Thomas Aquinas, to name only the most important. The construction of the church of St-Etienne-du-Mont began in 1492 and continued until 1622, when the facade was completed. It is impossible not to be struck by the originality of this church. The facade is a bizarre amalgamation of the Gothic and Renaissance styles, but its three superimposed pediments, because of their very peculiarity, succeed in creating a unified and coherent appearance. The church also contains the reliquary of the patron saint of Paris, St. Geneviève, who in 451 saved the city from the threat posed by the Huns. In Gothic style with three aisles and transept, the interior has soaring cylindrical piers which support the vaults and are linked together by a gallery above the arches. But the most picturesque part of the interior, which makes St. Etienne unique of its kind in Paris, is the *jubé*; that is, the suspended gallery which separates the nave from the choir. Possibly designed by Philibert Delorme, it is the only *jubé* known in Paris and its construction dates to 1521 to 1545 ca. The splendid fretwork of Renaissance inspiration with which it is decorated continues into the spiral staircases at the sides, thus creating an uninterrupted rhythmic effect. In the ambulatory next to the pillars of the Lady Chapel lie two great figures of 17th-century French literature: Pascal and Racine.

Hôtel de Cluny
(Musée National du Moyen Age)

Standing next to the ruins of the Roman baths (late 2nd to early 3rd century), this building–surrounded by green lawns and gardens–is one of the finest examples of International Gothic architecture in Paris. On this land, owned by the monastery of Cluny in Burgundy, the abbot Jacques d'Amboise had a building raised (1485-1498) as a residence for Benedictine monks who came from Cluny to visit the capital. During the Revolution, the building was decreed public property and was sold. In 1833 it became the residence of the collector Alexandre du Sommerand; at his death in 1842, his home and collections were acquired by the state. The museum, containing objects illustrating life in medieval France ranging from costumes to goldsmiths' wares, from majolica to weapons and armor, and from statues to tapestries, was inaugurated two years later.

The exterior and the interior of the beautiful church of Saint-Etienne-du-Mont.

The "Dame à la Licorne"

The series of tapestries that includes the "Dame à la Licorne" is one of the most celebrated and significant of the late Middle Ages. It is a group of six tapestries dating to the late 15th century intended as allegorical representations of the five senses. The tapestries were discovered in 1841 by Prosper Mérimée following the sale of the Château de Boussac in which they were hanging. Here, the writer George Sand saw and admired them and sang their beauty to the public at large in her novel *Jeanne*. Large (each is a near-square of about 3.5 meters per side) and unique as to meaning and compositive style, the tapestries are all woven of silk and wool threads. Each panel is an enchanted wood with thousands of flowers, populated by fantastic animals. At the center of each, a young woman is represented, each time in different clothing and a different pose: she holds a mirror, plays an organ, tastes a sweetmeat, binds a crown of flowers, caresses a unicorn, places a necklace in a coffer. The harmony of the chromatic range, the subtle and mysterious symbolism of the scenes, the poetic atmosphere, the great attention to detail, all contribute to making these tapestries true masterpieces of late medieval art. Over the tent is written "A Mon Seul Désir": scholars are still uncertain whether to attribute this inscription an introductory or a conclusive function in the context of the series.

The Musée National du Moyen Age (Cluny Museum) in the Hôtel de Cluny, and, top, the famous tapestry entitled "Dame à la Licorne".

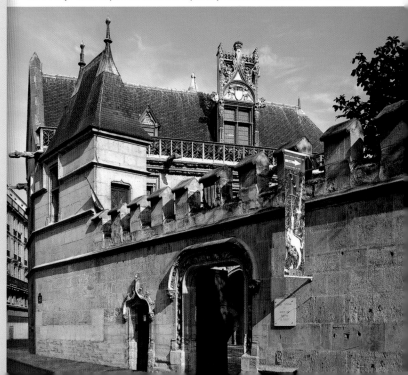

Eglise de la Sorbonne

The church of the Sorbonne is one of the oldest of the university buildings: constructed between 1635 and 1642 by Lemercier, its facade is typically Baroque, with two orders below an elegant cupola. The motif of the volutes which link the lower order to the upper is Italian in origin; a pictorial note is introduced by the passage from the columns in the lower part to the flatter pilaster strips in the upper part, which creates a gradual increase in luminosity. Inside the church, in the transept, is the white marble tomb of Cardinal Richelieu, sculpted by Girardon in 1694 to a design by Le Brun.

St-Julien-le-Pauvre

The small church of St-Julien-le-Pauvre is on Square René Viviani, where in 1620 there was planted a locust sapling (*Robinia pseudoacacia*) that is now one of Paris' oldest trees. The church was built between 1165 and 1220 ca. on the foundations of a pre-existing 6th-century building. Altered during the 17th century, the building was used as a depot for storing salt during the Revolution. Since 1889 it has been under the auspices of the Melkite Order, a congregation of Eastern Catholics who observe a Byzantine Rite.

Saint-Germain-des-Prés

Here one is emerged once more in the animated life of the quarter of St. Germain, whose typical and colorful streets interweave and cross to form picturesque corners. Here too is the church of Saint-Germain-des-Prés, the oldest church in Paris, built between the 11th and 12th centuries, destroyed no less than four times in forty years by the Normans, and each time rebuilt in its severe Romanesque forms. The facade incorporates the remains of the 12th-century portal, unfortunately half-hidden by the portico erected in 1607. The bell-tower, on the other hand, is entirely Romanesque, its corners reinforced by robust buttresses. In the 19th century, the two towers which stood at the sides of the choir were demolished, and of the choir itself there are only a few remains. The interior has three aisles and a transept, the end of which was modified in the 17th century. As a result of 19th-century restoration, the vaults and capitals are now so richly decorated to permit full appreciation of the otherwise simple and severe structure of the interior. The most interesting part of the building is the choir with its ambulatory, where the original architecture of the 12th century is still, in part, preserved intact. In this church are the tombs of two illustrious figures: René Descartes, in the second chapel on the right, and the Polish king John Casimir, in the transept on the left.

The Baroque facade of the Sorbonne Church and the severe Romanesque lines of Saint-Julien-le-Pauvre (left) and Saint-Germain-des-Prés (right).

Place des Vosges

Looking at it from above, from one of the typical dormer windows above the slate roofs, the square has the appearance of an enormous church cloister: perfectly square, 118 yards per side, it is completely closed in by thirty-six picturesque old buildings with porticoes on the ground floor, surmounted by two orders of windows. In the square itself are green trees and flower gardens, while in the center is a marble statue of Louis XIII on horseback, a copy of the original by P. Biard destroyed during the Revolution. The square, on the site of the Hôtel des Tournelles, where Henry II died in a tournament in 1559, was designed by Henry IV in 1607 and completed in 1612. Because of its perfect form, because of the succession of porticoes which must have lent themselves to tranquil promenades, and because of the gentle contrast between the green of the gardens and the severity of the surrounding buildings, the square became a center of fashionable life in that Paris which had not yet experienced the horror and violence of the Revolution. In the center of the southern side is the Pavilion of the King, the most splendid of the buildings, reserved for Henry IV, while facing it is the building occupied by the Queen. At no. 6 is the Victor Hugo Museum, occupying the house where the great writer lived from 1832 until 1848.

A view of Place des Vosges and, right, the facade of the Hôtel Salé, home of the Musée Picasso.

MUSÉE PICASSO - Inaugurated in 1985, the museum occupies the Hôtel Aubert de Fontenay in Rue de Thorigny, built in 1656 by J. Boullier. Its owner made his fortune collecting the salt tax; hence the mansion's nickname Hôtel Salé. Here is the famous exhibit of "Picasso's Picassos": the sculptures and paintings from which the great Spanish artist, who died in 1973, never wanted to be separated. There are over 200 paintings, 158 sculptures, 88 ceramics, over three thousand engravings and sketches, and an incredible number of letters, objects, photographs, and manuscripts. Then there

is Picasso's personal collection, previously at the Louvre: works by Cézanne, Renoir, Braque, Modigliani, and Matisse. Among the numerous works exhibited are *Self-Portrait in Blue* (1901), *Three Women under a Tree*, painted between 1907 and 1908, the *Great Nude in the Red Armchair*, the *Crucifixion* (1930), and the *Composition with Butterfly*, painted in 1932 and until recently thought to have disappeared. All of these works were given to the French government by the heirs of the Spanish genius as payment for succession duties on the properties owned by Picasso in France.

Musée Carnavalet

The museum is housed in two buildings joined by a corridor. The Hôtel Carnavalet, one of the finest in the city, was built in 1544 in Renaissance style and embellished with its lovely sculptural decoration by Jean Goujon; it was renovated in 1655 by François Mansart who added another story, making it what it is now. In 1677, the building was rented by the writer Marie de Rabutin, better known as the Marquise de Sévigné, and in the 19th century the Museum was opened. It contains historical documents of great importance and rarity related to the history of Paris, seen through its historical figures, monuments, and costumes, from Henry IV to our time.

Ceremony of Laying of the First Stone of the New Church of Sainte-Geneviève in 1763 (against a full-scale model of the new facade) in a painting by Pierre-Antoine Demachy (1723-1807).

Louis XIV and His Entourage Visiting the Church at the Hôtel Royal des Invalides on 14 July 1701 by Pierre-Denis Martin (1673-1742).

Portrait of Napoleon I, oil on canvas by Robert Lefèvre (1755-1830), painted in 1809.

Portrait of Juliette Récamier (1777-1849) by François Gérard (1770-1837).

A View of the Market and Fountain of the Innocents, painted in 1822 by John James Chalon (1778-1854).

After the Service at the Church of Holy Trinity, around 1900 by Jean Béraud (1849-1935).

The Oath of the Jeu de Paume, 20 June 1789, attributed to Jacques-Louis David (1748-1825).

The Republic as celebrated in two great Parisian squares: Place de la Nation (top) and Place de la République (bottom).

Place de la Nation

Originally Place du Trône, after the throne erected here on 26 August 1660, when Louis XIV and Maria Theresa made their entrance into the city. During the Revolution, when the guillotine was installed here, it was called Place du Trône Renversé; it took its present name in 1880. The bronze group of the *Triumph of the Republic*, by Dalou (1899), is set on the basin in the center of the square.

Place de la République

This vast rectangular plaza was created by Haussmann (1854) as an area for the maneuvers of the troops sent to put down the popular uprisings of the time. At the center stands the monument with the statue of the Republic (1883), set on a pedestal decorated with bronze bas-reliefs by Dalou depicting events in the history of the Republic.

Place de la Bastille

A massive fortress, built in 1370 for Charles V and finished in 1382, stood to the west of the present square. It was used thereafter as the state prison: one of its inmates was the mysterious figure who passed into history as the "Iron Mask." This melancholy fortress thus became the first and most

The Opéra Bastille, with its unmistakable curved facade.

important objective of the popular uprising that broke out on 14 July 1789, when several hundred enraged Parisians marched against what was considered the symbol of monarchic absolutism. Demolition of the fortress began the very next day; the job was finished the following year.

Today, an undulating line on the paving of the square, at the center of which stands the July Column, marks the perimeter of the ancient fortress.

At the back of the square stands the **Opéra Bastille**, designed by Carlos Ott, with its singular glass facade that curves around the main auditorium with its rotating stage. Inaugurated on 14 July 1989, on occasion of the Bicentennial of the French Revolution, the auditorium seats 2700 spectators.

The **July Column** (*Colonne de Juillet*) was erected in the years 1831 to 1840 to commemorate the Parisians killed during the revolt of July 1830. Their bodies, with those of the fallen in February 1848, are interred in the marble base, while their names are inscribed on the column shaft. Atop the column (access to which is up a 238-step staircase), at 52 meters above ground level, there stands a colossal figure of the *Génie de la Liberté* (Spirit of Liberty); the observation deck offers a marvelous panorama of the Marais quarter, of the Cité, and of the Sainte Geneviève hill.

Sacré-Cœur

The Prussian siege of Paris in 1870 was ultimately responsible for construction of this massive basilica that dominates Paris from the summit of the Montmartre hill: the population solemnly pledged to build a basilica if France were liberated from enemy occupation. The contest, called by the National Assembly in 1873, was won by the architect Paul Abadie, who had previously restored the Périgueux Cathedral. Construction was financed by public subscription in every parish in France, which collected 23 million francs of the time. The first stone was laid on 16 June 1875, but war postponed consecration of the church until 1919. The basilica's architects (among the most important were Abadie and Magne) designed it in a curious style, a blend of the Romanesque and the Byzantine. The four small domes and the large central dome, standing solidly on its high drum, are typically Oriental. At the rear, a square bell-tower 84 meters in height contains the famous "Savoyarde," a bell weighing no less than 19 tons–and thus one of the world's largest. Stately steps lead up to the facade of the church and the porch with three arches which stands in front; above are equestrian statues of what are perhaps France's two best-loved historical figures, King Louis the Blessed and Joan of Arc. The plastic, pictorial, and mosaic decoration of the

interior is often so incredibly elaborate as to mask and distort the architectural features. From the inside of the church, the visitor may descend into the vast underground crypt or else climb up to the top of the cupola to admire a panoramic view of the city and its surrounding areas extending for 50 kilometers. The white mass of the basilica itself is probably best viewed from Place St. Pierre below, accessible by a convenient cable-car or the ramps of stairs.

Three images of the Basilique du Sacré-Cœur: thanks to its dense grain, the facing stone from the Souppes quarries has always remained a pristine white.

Montmartre

Montmartre was and is one of the most picturesque quarters in Paris. Incorporated into the city of Paris in 1860, becoming the XVIII Arrondissement, Montmartre rises on a limestone hill at 130 m a.s.l. where, according to legend, Saint Denis (also called Dionysius), the first Bishop of Paris, was decapitated in 272 (hence the denomination *Mons Martyrum*—"hill of the martyr"—from which the current name derives). For the entire 19th century, Montmartre was a pole of attraction for all those artists for whom the bohemian style meant first of all living in freedom, making their art their principal raison de vivre, and rejecting all orthodox political and social viewpoints and outside impositions in general. Every painter who lived here, from the most famous to the least-known, has left a mark on Montmartre with the events of his life and his art.

At the foot of the hill (the *butte Montmartre*) is Place Blanche, dominated by the long vanes of the **Moulin Rouge**. The music hall, founded in 1889, has staged the art of Valentin le Désossé, the elegant and sophisticated Jane Avril, and La Goulue, the popular washerwoman who became the club's prima ballerina—and so many others. With the energetic and provocative can-can that was—and still is—performed on its stage, the Moulin Rouge is inseparably associated with the painter Henri de Toulouse-Lautrec, who spent many of his nights here and captured, with his crayon and brushes, the most intmate details and characteristic images, the most human and truest aspects of nightlife in the cabarets and theaters. The Moulin Rouge was the temple of those people whose lives played out in art but who, to Art (canonized art, consecrated by official recognition), were denied access.

© Moulin Rouge®

Two images of the picturesque Place du Tertre.

PLACE DU TERTRE – With its colors and the goings-on that animate it at all times of day and night, this ancient city square is the heart of Montmartre. In Place du Tertre, time has not stopped but has run ahead, welcoming new ideas and new personalities. With their souvenir shops, art galleries, typical restaurants, quaint cafés, Place du Tertre and the web of streets and alleys around it still offer a pinch of the atmosphere of times past. The portrait-painters who fill the square are there for the tourists, but their gestures, their concentration as they slowly daub their canvases, their poses on their stools or small iron seats facing their easels, are exactly the same as they were a century ago. There are no famous monuments in this small, tree-lined square: the monuments are the people themselves, the people who live and work here and fill the space with their colors and their voices.

And even if it is not "great art," anyone stopping here will take away a little bit of the city in an image, set to canvas or paper, immortalized in a few square centimeters: a memento that will never be just another souvenir but one more way of saying "I love Paris."

La Défense

Sprawling over 750 hectares, and still expanding, La Défense is Europe's largest business district. A vast plaza, the Parvis, 300 meters wide and 120 long, is closed in on three sides by the Grand Arche and the CNIT and Quatre Temps buildings: the latter is one of Europe's largest shopping malls. La Défense represents, in many respects, a synthesis of contemporary architecture, with its huge constructions in pure geometric forms: the Aveva (old Framatome, old Fiat), Manhattan, Gan, Total (previously Elf), and EDF towers, the latter by Pei Cobb Freed & Partners and 165 meters in height. The CNIT (Centre National des Industries et Techniques) building, a venue for great annual trade show events, was designed by the architects Zehrfuss, Camelot, and Mailly and built of concrete sails in a daring form that represents an upturned shell resting on only three supports.

The Grande Arche, the third largest in the city after the Carrousel and the Arc de Triomphe, which closes the long, triumphal Axe Historique.

La Grande Arche
Designed in 1982 by the Danish architect Johan Otto von Spreckelsen and inaugurated in July 1989, the Grande Arche is an enormous, emptied-out, almost perfect cube, 112 meters in height. At the center of the structure, which is faced in Carrara marble and glass, floats a sort of huge sail in Teflon fabric, steel, and glass entitled *Nuages*. Four elevators give access to the observation deck, which hosts an exhibit illustrating the construction of the arch.

La Villette

The Parc de la Villette (55 hectares) was created to house the Cité des Sciences et de l'Industrie. Here you'll find the *Géode*, a 36-meter diameter steel sphere created in 1985 by Adrien Fainsilber to house a hemispherical movie screen with a surface area of a thousand square meters; the Grande Halle, in glass and iron, dated 1867 and the only surviving structure of the three original slaughterhouses; the Zénith, a concert hall seating 6400; and the Cité de la Musique, which among other things hosts a museum dedicated to the history of European music from the Renaissance through our day.

Versailles

The palace and park of Versailles lie outside of Paris, about 20 kilometers to the southwest of the city. At the time of Louis XIII it was no more than a modest hunting lodge, built in 1624 and consisting of a simple building on a square plan with, at its center, what is today the Cour de Marbre (Marble Court). We owe creation of the grand Versailles palace to Louis XIV, who, following the Frondes civil disorders chose to abandon Paris and transform Versailles into a royal palace. In 1668, Le Vau doubled the existing building, adding a broad facade on the side facing the park. The work of transforming the palace went on for a long time under the direction of Hardouin-Mansart and then Le Nôtre, who handled mainly the layout of the grandiose gardens. When the royal family and the court were forced to return to Paris in October of 1789, the castle fell into a state of almost total disrepair; it was sacked more than once and many of its works of art were carried off. Finally, in 1837, Louis-Philippe restored it and made it a museum of French history. Versailles was occupied by the Germans in 1870, and it was here that Wilhelm of Prussia was crowned Emperor of Germany. In 1875, Versailles was the site of the proclamation of the Republic and in 1919 the peace treaty with Germany that ended World War I was signed here. Past the Grille d'Honneur ("gate of honor") is the first courtyard, the Cour des Ministres, at the end of which the equestrian statue of Louis XIV is set off by the two long buildings called the Ailes des Ministres or "Ministers' Wings"; the carriages of the royal family had access to the second courtyard, the Cour Royale, which is delimited to the right by the Aile Gabriel (after its designer) or

Aile Louis XV (for whom it was built) and to the left by the old left wing of the palace; and finally, the innermost courtyard, the Cour de Marbre, is embraced by the first nucleus of Louis XIII's castle with its red brick alternating with white stone. The three windows of the center balcony were those of the king's chamber, and it was here, on the first of September, 1715, at 8:15 a.m., that the death of Louis XIV was announced; 74 years later, on the same balcony, Louis XVI appeared to placate the population who demanded his return to Paris. The west facade of the palace is the best-known and the most beautiful, extending for 580 meters and opening on the harmonious palace gardens. Le Vau is responsible for the jutting central core, while the wings that backstep so elegantly were designed Hardouin-Mansart. Each portion of the building is composed on two orders, the lower with bossage arches and the upper with pillars and pilaster strips flanking high windows. The lower two orders are crowned by a balustraded attic floor, assigned as lodgings to the members of the court. The central core and the main floors of the two wings were, instead, for the use of the king's family and the royal princes.

The palace is home to the **Galeries de l'Histoire de France** (with 11 rooms illustrating the eras of Louis XIII and Louis XIV) and the **Opéra**, designed by Gabriel in 1770 for the marriage of Louis XVI to Marie-Antoinette: it is oval in form, with precious carved and gilded wood decoration against a blue background. Of note on the first floor, the Chapel Royal, built to bold plans by Hardouin-Mansart in the period 1698-1710, with a nave and two aisles and squared-

At the time of Louis XIV, the Galerie des Glaces—the Hall of Mirrors—was illuminated in the evening by three thousand candles.

off pilasters supporting the vaults, which in turn support a tribune with fluted columns. And on the same floor, the six halls of the Grand Apartment (Grand Appartement du Roi), richly appointed with stuccowork, polychrome marbles, and tapestries. It was here that the king received the court thrice weekly, from 6:00 to 10:00 in the evening. The rooms take their names from the various mythological subjects frescoed on the ceilings; thus, the Abundance Salon and the Venus

The Salon de la Guerre (Salon of War): in the monumental plaster medallion, Coysevox's Triumph of Louis XIV portrays the king in a heroic pose.

Right, the Salon de la Paix (Salon of Peace), which gives access to the Hall of Mirrors and the Queen's Bedchamber with its sumptuous decor.

Salon are followed by the Diana Salon (with Bernini's bust of Louis XIV), once the billiard room, and the Mars Salon, used as a ballroom, with the beautiful Gobelin tapestry of *Louis XIV Entering Dunkirk*; the Mercury Salon, used as a gaming room and where for eight days the corpse of Louis XIV lay in state; the Apollo Salon, a music room that during the day doubled as throne room. By far, the most opulent of the palace halls is the celebrated Hall of Mirrors (Galerie des Glaces), a masterpiece by Hardouin-Mansart who began construction in 1678 (it was terminated eight years later). Seventy-five meters long by ten wide, with its vaulted ceiling adorned by Le Brun with paintings illustrating French victories, the hall has 17 broad windows overlooking the park and matching the same number of arcaded mirrors on the opposite wall. Among the many precious furnishings and decorations in the Hall were tapestries, statues, and orange trees in pots of solid silver. The smaller King's Suite (Appartement du Roi) included the Council Cabinet, where Louis XIV usually worked with his ministers, the Bedchamber, paneled in white wood and gold, and the Œil-de-Bœuf Salon, where every morning and every evening the court dignitaries awaited the king's rising and his preparations for his night's repose. The Queen's Suite (Grand Appartement de la Reine), built in 1671-1680, consisted of the Bedchamber, the Peers' Salon, the Antechamber (with beautiful Gobelins tapestries and a portrait of Marie-Antoinette by Vigée-Lebrun), and the

Queen's Guards Room, where on 6 October 1789 a group of rebels from Paris massacred several of the guards who defended Marie-Antoinette. Six other small rooms in pure Louis XIV style form the so-called "Petits Appartements" where Marie-Antoinette sought refuge from royal life.
Of particular note among the other rooms is the Galerie des Batailles, created by Louis-Philippe in 1836 and once his bedroom, which takes its name from the paintings illustrating the most famous battles in the history of France.
Gardens – With their elegant style, artistic contrivances, and striking inventions, the gardens of Versailles are considered the prototype of the French formal garden. An integral part of the palace, occupying an area of 100 hectares, the gardens were designed between 1661 and 1668 by Le Nôtre, who involved the king in their planning and astounded him with his genial imagination, creating and re-creating nature, planting and orchestrating trees, wooded patches, and hedgerows. Sculptural groups in marble and bronze and fountains spurting jets of water on high are to be found everywhere. From the central terrace, the visitor descends to the Leto Basin, a masterpiece by Marsy portraying the goddess with her children Diana (Artemis) and Apollo, that triumphs over the concentric pools that rise in pyramidal form. This fountain marks the start of the long boulevard called the Tapis-Vert that leads to the great Pool of Apollo: its creator, Tuby, imagined the god's chariot drawn by four horses

The Mars Salon, used as a music room for court soirées.

Right, the fountain with the sculptural group of Leto and her children.

that rise imperiously from the waters to illuminate the sky, while the Tritons blow their shell trumpets to announce the arrival of Apollo.

A further example of the luxury and the opulent life-style at Versailles are the Trianons. The Grand Trianon was erected by Mansart in 1687 in the classical forms of an Italian-style palace. Inside, Napoleon I's reception rooms (in which his favorites Maintenon and Pompadour had previously lived), and the apartment of Louis XIV, where the king lived from 1703 until his death. The Petit Trianon, instead, built by Gabriel, is known as the "palace of the favorites" of France. With its simple facade, lightened by columns, and its elegant style and harmonious proportions, the small palace may be considered the first true example of the Neoclassical style. In the surrounding garden, a "Temple of Love," with 12 Corinthian-style columns supporting the dome that shelters a statue of *L'Amour Captif de la Jeunesse*, and the "Hamlet of the Queen," or Hameau, an evocative snatch of faux countryside with thatched cottages, a dairy with cows, and a water-mill once driven by a stream. Conceived by Richard Mique and Hubert Robert, this was Marie-Antoinette's favorite spot for strolling.

INDEX